THE BEILIS TRANSCRIPTS

THE BEILIS TRANSCRIPTS

The Anti-Semitic Trial that Shook the World

Ezekiel Leikin

JASON ARONSON INC.
Northvale, New Jersey
London

All photos are from the Archives of the YIVO Institute for Jewish Research.

This book was set in 11 pt. Cheltenham by Lind Graphics of Upper Saddle River, New Jersey, and printed by Haddon Craftsmen in Scranton, Pennsyvlania.

Library of Congress Cataloging-in-Publication Data

The Beilis transcripts : the anti-semitic trial that shook the world / [translated and edited] by Ezekiel Leikin.
    p. cm.
    Includes bibliographical references and index.
    ISBN 0-87668-179-8
    1. Beilis, Mendel, 1874–1934—Trials, litigation, etc. 2. Trials (Murder)—Ukraine—Kiev. 3. Blood accusation. 4. Antisemitism--Russia—History—20th century. I. Leikin, Ezekiel.
KLP41.B45B45 1993
345.47′71402523—dc20
[344.7714052523]   92-39643

Manufactured in the United States of America. Jason Aronson Inc. offers books and cassettes. For information and catalog write to Jason Aronson Inc., 230 Livingston Street, Northvale, New Jersey 07647.

For George

Contents

Photo section begins after page 138.

Preface

This volume offers a factual account of the Beilis case, a ritual-murder accusation against Jews in czarist Russia, which—along with the Dreyfus case in France—ranks among the most famous anti-Semitic trials in modern history.

A number of noteworthy books have been written about the Beilis case—and I have relied extensively upon the insights, research, and data embodied therein. What makes this volume unique is that it provides, in abbreviated form, the "chemistry" of the Beilis trial itself—the testimony of the witnesses, the verbal clashes between the prosecution and defense teams, the speeches of the accusers and the defenders, and the ambience of the czarist court. I have also attempted to show the sinister schemes hatched behind the scenes by ministers and high officials of the czarist government, with the tacit approval of Czar Nicholas II, to prove the veracity of the blood-libel accusation and thus defame and slander Jews and Judaism.

My principal source for the trial proceedings was the actual court transcript. The supplementary data were drawn from books referred to in the References. Numerous witnesses were called on to testify at the trial, but I have selected only those whose testimony was substantive. As for the speeches for the prosecution and the defense, I have chosen the major presentations, inasmuch as the speeches by Shmakov (for the prosecution) and Karabchevsky and Zarudny (for the defense) were highly repetitive. By all accounts, the speeches by Gruzenberg and Maklakov (defense) and Vipper and Zamislovski (prosecution) were deemed to have been the most incisive and articulate. In fact, some of the jurors revealed that they were especially impressed with Maklakov's brilliant exposition.[1]

The court transcripts of the Beilis trial, which I was able to salvage from my father's once-vast library, have intrigued and fascinated me for many years. At least once a year, I was in the habit of picking up one of the transcript volumes. I found myself being transposed into the milieu of a Russian court in Kiev, where a real-life drama revolving around a ritual murder accusation against Jews was being staged by high officials of a government on the brink of collapse.

It was the time frame of the trial that endowed it with an aura of surrealism. Rooted, as it was, on an ancient, long-demolished myth—the blood libel—the Beilis drama might have received rave reviews in the Middle Ages. The fact that it was staged in the twentieth century, in the country of Tolstoy, Chekhov, and Gorky— to name but a few of Russia's "greats"—is perhaps what makes the Beilis trial so hauntingly fascinating to a contemporary student of history.

---

1. Maurice Samuel, *Blood Accusation—The Strange History of the Beilis Case* (Philadelphia: Jewish Publication Society, 1966), p. 178.

Acknowledgments

For his encouragement and inspiration, I am grateful to my friend and mentor, Philip Slomovitz, founder and editor emeritus of the Detroit Jewish News and dean of the American English-Jewish Press.

I am indebted to my good friend, Professor Leon H. Warshay of Detroit's Wayne State University, for his generous assistance in locating books I found valuable in researching the Beilis case.

Introduction
A Brief History of the Blood Libel

The blood-libel accusation first surfaced in 1144 in England, when the dead body of a young boy, William, was found in a wood near Norwich. The child apparently lost consciousness as a result of a cataleptic fit and was buried prematurely. Word got around that he was murdered by Jews for ritual purposes. The body was exhumed and reburied in a solemn ceremony at the city's cathedral, while mobs began roaming the city, seeking revenge against the murderous Jews. A massacre was prevented by the sheriff, who allowed the Jews to seek shelter in the royal castle. Notwithstanding this measure, one of the leading members of the Jewish community was murdered. The young boy who had died was beatified as a martyr and became known as St. William of Norwich. Thereafter, instances of mob violence against Jews recurred with increasing frequency in England and the continent. Exposed and repudiated as a hoax by the popes and many theologians, the canard that the Jewish religion and its sacred books—including the Bible and the Talmud—prescribe the use of Christian blood, generally that of a child, for ritual purposes gained currency and was disseminated and promoted by anti-Semites worldwide.

History records a stirring repudiation of this calumny by Rabbi Menasseh Ben Israel of Amsterdam in pleading before Oliver Cromwell in 1657 for the readmission of the Jews to England, and repeated by Britain's chief rabbi, Solomon Hershell, at the time of the Damascus blood accusation in 1840:

> I swear, without any deceit or fraud, by the most high God, the creator of heaven and earth, who promulgated his law to the people of Israel upon Mount Sinai, that I never yet to this day saw any such custom among the people of Israel, and that they do not hold any such thing by divine precept of the law, or any ordinance or institution of their wise men, and that they never committed or endeavored such wickedness, and if I lie in this matter, then let all the curses mentioned in Leviticus and Deuteronomy come upon me, let me never see the blessings and consolation of Zion, nor attain to the resurrection of the dead.

The earliest papal pronouncement on the blood libel was occasioned by a ritual-murder accusation in southern France in 1247. In an encyclical addressed to the archbishops and bishops of Germany and France, Pope Innocent IV declared:

> Nor shall anyone accuse them [the Jews] of using human blood in their religious rights, since in the Old Testament they are instructed not to use blood of any kind, let alone human blood. But since at Fulda and in several other places many Jews were killed on the grounds of such suspicion, we, by the authority of those present, strictly forbid that this should be repeated in future. If anyone knowing the tenor of this decree should, God forbid, dare to oppose it, he shall be punished by loss of his rank and office, or be placed under a sentence of excommunication, unless he makes proper amends for his presumption.

However, undeterred by these strictures, the calumny continued to gain credence and fueled anti-Jewish excesses on an ever larger scale. In 1840, the Damascus blood accusation attracted international attention and involved the intervention of several European powers. Under Islam, blood accusations against Jews were unknown. It was only in the nineteenth century, when French traders and missionaries "imported" the European strain of anti-Semitism into Moslem lands, that this calumny surfaced in the Near East.

In February 1840 in Damascus, an Italian Capuchin monk and his servant vanished without a trace. Fellow monks spread the charge that they were murdered by Jews for ritual purposes. Sharif Pasha, the governor, ordered the arrest of a Jewish barber, who promptly confessed and implicated seven leading members of the Jewish community as the instigators of the murder. Other Jews were arrested, and they also confessed. The news spread, and the local Jewish community was subjected to mob violence. It was soon established that the confessions were extracted under torture, which put the guilt of those accused in doubt. The situation was further aggravated by the intervention of the French consul in Damascus on the side of the accusers, with the blessings of the French government in Paris. The consul's involvement was attributed to French-British rivalry in the Middle East; thus, Britain denounced the accusations and the United States followed suit and lodged a formal protest. Two prominent Jews, Adolphe Cremieux of France and Moses Montefiore of Britain, met with the sultan, whereupon the latter issued an official denunciation of the charge of ritual murder by Jews. Historian Cecil Roth observed that the outcome of the Damascus affair was "a victory for Jews not only because of its triumphant issue, but because it was the starting-point of a new solidarity between the Jews of various countries."[1]

Between 1887 and 1900, twenty-two anti-Jewish incidents of violence were recorded in Europe, of which the most notorious were the Tisza-Eszlar affair in Hungary, Xanen on the Rhineland,

---

1. Cecil Roth, quoted in Albert S. Lindemann, *The Jew Accused—Three Anti-Semitic Affairs (Dreyfus, Beilis, Frank 1894–1915)* (Cambridge: Cambridge University Press, 1991), p. 38.

and Koenitz in Prussia. In Poland and Russia, ritual murder charges increased alarmingly in the nineteenth and twentieth centuries, decimating countless Jewish communities. By the end of the nineteenth century, under the reign of Czar Alexander III and his brilliant but rabidly anti-Semitic chief advisor, Pobedonostsev, pogroms became an integral part of government policy. Pobedonostsev devised a simple formula for solving "the Jewish problem": one-third would be forced to emigrate, one-third would be killed, and the one-third that remained would be converted.

On Easter of 1881, some of the most gruesome of a series of pogroms erupted in southern Russia. Some one hundred Jewish communities were struck almost simultaneously. As the police stood idly by, masses of Jews were massacred and maimed and their possessions plundered. Under Nicholas II, who was czar from 1894 to 1917 and who viewed Jews as Christ-killers, the reign of terror continued unabated. The Kishinev pogrom in 1903—well planned and organized—surpassed all previous assaults in barbarity. It lasted for three days and ended on orders from St. Petersburg only after a wave of protests from many Western countries discomfited the czarist hierarchy. Several groups, organized with the blessings and patronage of the czar, were charged with the responsibility of planning and implementing the pogroms—"to strike fear in the Jewish population," to accelerate the process of russification (conversion) and forced emigration, and to destabilize and disrupt every manifestation of organized Jewish activity. Foremost among these groups was the Union of the Russian People and its assault troops, the Black Hundred. Count Witte, the foremost statesman of the time, referred to the membership of the Black Hundred as "the embodiment of nihilistic patriotism, feeding on lies, deceit, slander, savage and cowardly desperation ... mostly dark minded, the leaders are unhanged villains."[2] Other like-minded organizations, such as the Association of the Archangel Michael and the Double-

---

2. Maurice Samuel, *Blood Accusation—The Strange History of the Beilis Case* (Philadelphia: Jewish Publication Society, 1966), p. 19.

Headed Eagle (the latter gaining notoriety during the Beilis trial), were supportive of the Union's agenda and participated in its hate-mongering activities.

Russia at that time contained the bulk of the world's Jewish populace. The Jews' domicile was restricted to certain provinces, known as the Pale of Settlement; they were subjected to exorbitant, special taxes, and their children's access to institutions of higher learning was circumscribed by a rigid quota system.

Many young Jews cast their lot with the liberal and revolutionary segments of Russian society in the hope that radical reforms in the political system would bring them relief. Thus, next to "exploitation" and "parasitism," the Jews were accused of being the masterminds of the revolutionary movement, which, in the reactionary climate of the time, was tantamount to an affront to the czar himself.

Not all segments of Russian society were acquiescent in the country's treatment of its Jewish minority. Liberal circles, members of the intelligentsia, and such intellectual leaders as Tolstoy, Gorky, Korolenko, and others lashed out publicly against the government's Judeophobia, and particularly against the atrocities committed during the Kishinev pogrom. But their voices were drowned out by the clamorous anti-Semitic campaign fueled by the Union of the Russian People and its cohorts in the Black Hundred.

A new wave of pogroms erupted in 1905 in connection with the outbreak of the first revolution. Some 660 Jewish communities were terrorized in a single week, including Odessa, an important intellectual center of Russian Jewry, where three hundred Jews lost their lives and forty thousand—having been robbed of their possessions—were driven to poverty. This time, however, the pogromists met with stiff resistance from newly organized Jewish self-defense units. Determined to shed their previous passivity, Jewish youth, now politically more sophisticated and ideologically motivated, formed defensive units to resist the pogromists. These units would have been a match for the marauding rabble, were it not for the intervention of the military and the police, some of whom participated in the killing and looting. Apart from the constant incitement to physical violence, the government sought to tarnish the image of the Jews by means of the press and a large volume of anti-Semitic publications. Thus, during the years from 1905 to 1916, the government authorized the printing and dissemination of more than fourteen million copies of some twenty-eight hundred anti-Semitic books and pamphlets. The czar himself contributed over twelve million rubles toward the publication of the slanderous literature, including the printing of what was to become an anti-Semitic "classic," known as the "Protocols of the Elders of Zion." This notorious fabrication was first published in Russia in 1903, but it became a major sensation in 1920 when right-wing Russian extremists brought it to the West. In 1921 Herman Bernstein, an American journalist and former diplomat, published the *History of a Lie*, showing that the Protocols were modeled on an episode in a German novel called *Biarritz*, authored by a shady journalist, Herman Goedsche. Six months later, a correspondent of the *London Times*, Phillip Graves, revealed that large parts of the Protocols had been taken from Maurice Joly's "Dialogue in Hell between Machiavelli and Montesquieu," a satire on Napoleon III published in Brussels in 1864. In 1901 an obscure mystic, Sergius Nilus, published a religious book, *The Great in Little—the Coming of the Anti-Christ and the Rule of Satan on Earth.* In 1905, the Nilus book was reprinted by the czarist government press, and the Protocols were added as a commentary to the Nilus book. Notwithstanding the documented proof of their spuriousness, the Protocols continued to be printed and disseminated in many countries. In Nazi Germany they served as a blueprint for Hitler's war against the Jews. In *Mein Kampf* Hitler wrote, "The extent to which the whole existence of the Jewish people is based on a continual lie, is shown in an incomparable manner in the 'Protocols of the Elders of Zion.' " The central theme of the Protocols is an alleged Jewish conspiracy to take over the world. Some versions of this literary crazy quilt linked the World Zionist Congress to the Elders of Zion, whose meetings in Basel, Switzerland, in 1897 were allegedly designed to chart a master plan for world domination. Other plagiarized segments accused the Jewish Socialist Bund and the Freemasons of being partners in this mythical cabal. As paradoxical as it may seem, the Protocols had only a marginal effect upon the anti-Semitic campaign under the czar; it was during the successor regime of the Communists, under Stalin, that the Protocols were resurrected to become the most formidable weapon in the Soviet Union's arsenal against Judaism and "imperialist Zionism."

How pervasive the malignant effects of the forgery have been is illustrated in an episode referred to by Chaim Weizmann, the first president of Israel, in his memoirs.

Weizmann came to Palestine in 1918 as head of a Zionist commission sent by the British government to oversee the implementation of the Balfour Declaration in favor of a Jewish homeland.

"In an early conversation with General Wyndham Deedes . . . , I learned at least one source of our tribulations," he wrote. The general handed Weizmann a few sheets of typewritten script and asked him to read it. "I read the first sheet, asking him what could be the meaning of all this rubbish." Deedes replied, "You had better read all of it with care; it is going to cause you a great deal of trouble in the future." The typewritten sheets were extracts from the Protocols of the Elders of Zion. When Weizmann asked Deedes how the material reached him, he replied, "You will find it in the haversacks of a great many British officers here—and they believe it. It was brought over by the British Military Mission which has been serving in the Caucasus on the staff of the Grand Duke Nicholas."[3] It didn't take long for General Deedes's warning to assume a prophetic dimension. After World War II and the emergence of the State of Israel, Arab potentates were handing out copies of the Protocols to visiting dignitaries to show what they were up against, namely, not merely a tiny, upstart Jewish state dwarfed by a vast Moslem world, but a sinister Jewish plot of global dimensions.

The Protocols found receptive audiences throughout the world—

---

3. Chaim Weizmann, quoted in Samuel, *Blood Accusation*, p. 260.

in Japan, the Middle East, Africa, America, and, of course, Europe, where this myth was initially spawned.

The United States, too, was not immune to this pestilence. The Protocols found willing publishers in the United States and had succeeded in landing an important "client." Henry Ford and his mouthpiece, the *Dearborn Independent*, a rabidly anti-Semitic publication, purchased the Protocols and used them as a basis for their series against the Jewish people and Judaism. The American press treated the slanders of the *Dearborn Independent* as the ravings of bigots and hate mongers.

A convention of the Federal Council of Churches of Christ in America, in 1920, representing thirty denominations and fifty thousand churches, adopted a resolution deploring the "cruel and unwarranted attacks upon the Jews," which are "arousing racial division in our body politic." In July 1927, Henry Ford recanted his Jew-baiting activities and made a public apology to the Jewish people.

"I am deeply mortified," he declared, "that this journal (*The Dearborn Independent*) has been made the medium for resurrecting exploded fictions and for giving currency to the so-called Protocols of the Elders of Zion, which have been demonstrated to be gross forgeries." The crude, primitive strain of European anti-Semitism failed to take root in America. Yet, in spite of public aversion to all forms of prejudice and bigotry based on race and religion, anti-Jewish incidents linked to the blood libel occurred intermittently in several American cities. One incident in particular, which stirred up anti-Jewish passions in the course of a sensational trial reminiscent of the Beilis case, took place in Atlanta, Georgia, in 1913—the year Beilis's acquittal was announced in Kiev, Russia.

On April 27, 1913, fourteen-year-old Mary Phagan was found murdered in the basement of a pencil factory managed by a Jew, Leo Frank. In a lengthy, contentious trial, Leo Frank was found guilty of the murder, and while awaiting legal initiatives toward a new trial, his cell was broken into by a mob calling itself Knights of Mary Phagan, and he was abducted and was hanged from a tree.

The lynching evoked a storm of indignation throughout the country. Initially, Leo Frank's arrest and conviction had not been construed as motivated by anti-Semitism. Indeed, five Jews served on the jury that indicted him. However, as the trial progressed, agitation in the press, exacerbated by political rivalry among Atlanta's political leaders, focused on "Jewish money" and "northern Jewish influence" as the malignant forces trying to subvert "southern justice." Moreover, the galaxy of prominent lawyers enlisted to defend Frank consistently belabored the theme that the defendant was the victim of rampant anti-Semitism and that he would have never been convicted in a northern court on the basis of the flimsy evidence produced against him.

The specter of a blood-libel accusation against Jews also arose in a small town in New York State in 1928. "Massena," according to historian Saul S. Friedman, "was a volcano of economic jealousy . . . fanaticism, anti-Semitism, anti-Catholicism, anti-alienism and assorted other mesozoic hatreds. All that was needed to release the pent-up fury was an excuse."[4]

Barbara Griffiths, age four, was sent by her parents to fetch Bobby, her brother, who had gone into the woods with a neighbor to get willow branches with which to make whistles. Her brother emerged from the woods a few minutes after Barbara left. The parents were not particularly worried, expecting Barbara to return before dusk. When—at suppertime—the girl did not return, the father, Dave Griffiths, went looking for her. A search party, augmented by troopers of the state police and neighbors, continued to search through the night, but without success. Rumor spread through town that little Barbara had been murdered by Jews, who needed her blood for rites connected with the upcoming Yom Kippur holiday. The source of the rumor was Albert Comnas, a Greek immigrant who ran an ice cream parlor and cafe in town, whose bias against Jews was well known. It seems that one of the

---

4. Saul S. Friedman, *The Incident at Massena* (New York: Stein & Day, 1937), p. 29.

state troopers involved in the search for Barbara was taking his meals at Comnas's cafe, and the owner was ready to be helpful: "The Jews are having a holiday, maybe they need blood." On October 4, 1928, the *New York Post* wrote, "After all the efforts to find the child failed, the investigators began to work on the theory that possibly some person or persons had kidnapped the child and destroyed her . . . the first person to be investigated was the Jewish boy, Jacob Shaulkin." (The name of the boy was really Willie Shulkin, the mentally retarded son of Jacob Shulkin.) Massena's mayor, W. Gilbert Hawes, did not take the Jewish "connection" lightly. He ordered Trooper Mickey McCann, who was in charge of the search team, to verify the rumor. McCann and several idlers milling around the fire station entered a Jewish-owned clothing store and demanded to see the basement. Finding nothing incriminating, they proceeded to inspect other Jewish business establishments. Leaders of the Jewish community, disturbed by the escalating agitation, which had the tacit support of the local authorities, decided to seek the counsel of Louis Marshall, nationally known Jewish leader and prominent attorney who lived in New York City. Marshall called on Boris Smolar, head of the Jewish Telegraphic Agency, to proceed forthwith to Massena to assess the situation on the spot. The girl was still missing—twelve hours after she had disappeared in the woods—and the search parties were still combing the surrounding areas. In the meantime, a group of vigilantes, many of whom were members of the Ku Klux Klan, assembled at city hall to await developments. Fear and anxiety gripped the Jewish community. Jews who had emigrated from Eastern Europe recalled with trepidation the consequences of the "blood accusations" in their native lands. The rabbi of the community, Berel Brennglass, was summoned to city hall, where a crowd of three to four hundred people were milling about in a "state of unusual excitement."

State trooper McCann interrogated the rabbi:

McCann: "Can you give any information as to whether your people in the Old Country offer human sacrifices?

RABBI BRENNGLASS (indignant): I am surprised that an officer of the United States, which is the most enlightened country in the world, should dare to ask such a foolish and ridiculous question.

McCANN: Was there ever a time when the Jewish people used human blood?

RABBI BRENNGLASS: No, never, that is a slander against the entire Jewish people.

McCANN: Please don't think the idea originated with me; somebody else, a foreigner, impressed me with it.[5]

At a subsequent meeting at the rabbi's home, it was decided to send urgent messages to Rabbi Stephen S. Wise, head of the American Jewish Congress, in New York; Lieutenant E. F. Heim, McCann's immediate superior; and again to Louis Marshall. The message was invariably the same. "We do not know how to proceed, we request that you immediately inform us what action to take." As the meeting was about to break up, Boris Smolar arrived from New York. Immediately thereafter, a group of Jews burst into the house shouting, "The child has been found. The child is alive." When she reached home, a large and jubilant crowd came to greet the missing girl. Her story was simple: looking for her brother in the woods and failing to find him, she crawled into the tall grass when it grew dark and fell asleep. After she awoke, she got lost on her way home, until she met two older girls from town, who brought her home. Boris Smolar reported, "The joy of the Jewish community was indescribable." The incident, however, did not end there. As the Jews were gathering for the Kol Nidre service that evening, their path was blocked by a mob that greeted them with such taunts as "Scared you into returning the girl, didn't we?"

Rabbi Brennglass's sermon that night, in which he excoriated the city government and the Ku Klux Klan "hoodlums," ended with the admonition, "We must forgive, but we must never forget, we must

---

5. Friedman, *Incident*, p. 118.

remind ourselves that this happened in America, not czarist Russia, among people we have come to regard as our friends."[6]

Mayor Hawes offered a halfhearted apology to the Jewish community, which the local leaders considered inadequate. Following the intervention of Louis Marshall and Rabbi Wise, Major John Warner, superintendent of the state police and Governor Al Smith's son-in-law, summoned the parties to Albany, where the Massena "incident" was threshed out. Just prior to the Albany meeting, Governor Smith, the Democratic candidate for the United States presidency, advised Rabbi Wise, "As Governor of the State, I cannot believe that this libelous myth has been resurrected and credited even for a moment by anyone connected with the service of the State, or any of its civil divisions. . . . I wish to assure you that I will see to it that this matter be investigated in the most thorough manner."[7] The matter was finally resolved with Major Hawes issuing a full and contrite apology, Trooper McCann being suspended and subsequently reassigned, and the City of Massena garnering national notoriety for succumbing to a libelous religious myth.

The extent to which the situation of the Jews in the United States has been "exceptional" is succinctly assessed by two historians. John Higham writes: "No decisive event, no deep crisis, no powerful social movement, no great individual is associated primarily with anti-Semitism."[8] Jonathan Sarna observes: If the United States "has not been utter heaven for Jews, it has been as far from Hell as Jews in the Diaspora have ever known."[9]

---

6. Friedman, *Incident*, p. 135.

7. Ibid., p. 155.

8. John Higham, quoted in Leonard Dinnerstein, ed., *Anti-Semitism in the United States* (New York, 1971), pp. 63–77.

9. Jonathan D. Sarna, "Anti-Semitism and American History," *Commentary* 71: 3 (March 1981), p. 47.

1

Introduction to the Beilis Trial

On Saturday, March 12, 1911, 13-year-old Andrey Yushchinsky left his home in Slobodka, a suburb of Kiev, ostensibly to go to school. Eight days later, his mangled body was discovered in a cave in the Lukyanovka section of Kiev.

It was ascertained that on March 12, Andrey decided to skip school and pay a visit to his friend Zhenya Cheberyak, whose mother, Vera Cheberyak, had achieved notoriety in the neighborhood as a fence and associate of known criminals.

Preliminary hearings before magistrates revealed that Andrey and Zhenya Cheberyak were observed that day walking leisurely halfway between the Cheberyak home and the Zaitsev brick factory, where Mendel Beilis worked as a clerk and dispatcher. At Andrey's funeral, leaflets were distributed, accusing Jews of the boy's murder and summoning the "Christian masses" to avenge "Andrey's martyrdom."

Initially, leaks from the police department and the press hinted that Andrey's relatives were involved in the crime, but as the

investigation progressed, Vera Cheberyak and her coterie of underworld associates emerged as the prime suspects. However, the
anti-Semitic organizations, notably the Union of the Russian People
and the Double-Headed Eagle, continued to point the finger of
blame at the Jews, urging the authorities to seek the culprits among
the city's "Yids."

In response to this anti-Semitic clamor, reinforced by similiar
"guidelines" from officials of the Ministry of Justice, Mendel Beilis
was taken into custody and indicted as a participant in the crime.

The Beilis trial, which took place in the city of Kiev, capital of the
Ukraine, in 1913, ranks—along with the Dreyfus Affair in France—
as one of the most notorious trials in modern history.

The trial was, in fact, a major conspiracy conceived by high
echelons of the government of Czar Nicholas II, fueled by the
reactionary, monarchist elements in Russian society and imple-
mented by officials of the Ministry of Justice with the tacit encouragement and approval of the czar. Following the revolution of 1905,
Russia was in the grip of a chauvinistic counterrevolution, of which
the Jews were the major scapegoats and victims. A rash of pogroms
unleashed by the rabidly anti-Semitic Union of the Russian People
and its shock troops, the Black Hundred, was symptomatic of this
period. The pretext for these officially inspired attacks against the
Jews was the blood libel, a long-discredited accusation that the
Jewish religion prescribes the use of Christian blood for ritualistic
purposes.

This fabrication, dating back to the Middle Ages, was a modified
version of an accusation leveled against the early Christians by the
Romans. Although it was denounced by the Vatican, as well as
countless scholars and theologians, as a baseless hoax, it nevertheless persisted into modern times. In Russia, the idea of the blood
libel was widely promoted and disseminated among the benighted
masses as a basic Jewish ritual linked to the Passover holiday,
because Christian blood was ostensibly required for use in the
baking of *matzos*. The czarist regime used the blood-libel charge as
a convenient political weapon to divert the attention of the masses

from the corrupt and repressive policies of the government and blame the Jews for all the ills besetting the empire. In its repeated attempts to put a political gloss upon the persecution of the Jews, the government called public attention to the "disproportionate" involvement of Jews in revolutionary movements, so as to characterize the pogroms as "outbursts of popular indignation."

The revolutionary movement, however, was growing in scope and intensity and was becoming increasingly unmanageable. The reactionary monarchist elements in the government were on the lookout for a new diversionary ploy to offset the revolutionary ferment agitating Russian society. It is in this context that the stage was set for the Beilis trial.

The Beilis Defense Team

Recruited to defend Beilis were some of Russia's most celebrated jurists. Heading the team was Oscar Gruzenberg, the foremost Jewish criminal lawyer of his generation. A proud, fearless man, he had defended many Jews and non-Jews for alleged crimes against the government, which did not endear him to the czarist hierarchy. He was as temperamental as he was gifted, and he was an acknowledged master at cross-examination. Among his clients were such luminaries as Maxim Gorky, Korolenko, and Leon Trotsky. In defending unjustly accused Jews, he was not content to redress wrongs done to them as individuals; he also tried to vindicate Jewish honor. Jews called him "the national defender." Gruzenberg was also active in political life and was named to the advisory council to the Third and Fourth Dumas (Constituent Assembly). During the Russian Civil War, he headed the Jewish Council for Self-Defense and the Council for Aiding the Victims of Pogroms.

After the Soviets came to power, Gruzenberg left Russia and spent the last years of his life in France.

N. B. Karabchevsky, another member of the defense team, was known as "the old lion" of the Russian bar. However, the outstanding member of the team was undoubtedly Vassily Maklakov, who besides being a brilliant attorney, was equally prominent in literature and science. After the 1917 revolution, he was appointed by the provisional government to be Russia's ambassador to France. It was the consensus among those monitoring the Beilis trial that his summation outshone his colleagues' presentations.

The youngest of the team was A. S. Zarudny, an intellectual with a quixotic temperament who frequently challenged the rulings of the presiding judge.

Grigorevich-Barsky, a prominent member of the Kiev bar, was enlisted as a member of the team because of his familiarity with local court procedures and practices.

The Accusers

The ablest of the accusers was G. G. Zamislovski, a member of the Duma and a prolific pamphleteer, mostly in defense of the monarchy and in inflammatory diatribes against Jews. He was privy to the inner-circle consultations of the notorious Union of the Russian People and close advisor to the Minister of Justice, I. G. Shcheglovitov.

S. Shmakov, the other civil prosecutor, was an old man and a connoisseur of anti-Semitic literature. His ramblings throughout the trial were laced with pseudoscientific quotations and references to obscure authors of Judeophobia. The state prosecutor, O. V. Vipper, a German, was an arrogant, foppish man who treated witnesses with cynical condescension and tried very hard to measure up to his more prominent colleagues with a display of unbridled contempt for Jews.

Mendel Beilis

Mendel Beilis, thirty-nine years old at the time of his trial, was an ex-soldier and the father of five children. He was employed as a dispatcher at the Zaitsev brick factory, having worked there for fifteen years. Kiev, his place of residence and the site of the trial, had a Jewish population of approximately twenty thousand, out of a total population of four hundred thousand. It was through his father, a pious Jew and a *hasid* who had some contact with the millionaire Jonas Zaitsev, an equally observant Jew, that Beilis got his job at the brick factory. His pay was forty-five rubles a month and free quarters, which qualified him for lower-middle-class status. Jonas Zaitsev died in 1907 and Beilis's hoped-for promotion to manager of the factory remained unfulfilled. He had little learning, although he could recite the Hebrew prayers and had some knowledge of common religious rites. He could read and write Yiddish, but spoke Russian poorly.

He worked regularly on the Sabbath and the Holy Days, except Rosh Hashanah and Yom Kippur. He sent his son to the local Gimnasia (high school), though to do so he had to sell his cow, while his wife took in boarders.

He worked from sunrise to sunset, checking the brick shipments, keeping accounts, and performing a variety of other chores. It may seem strange in retrospect, but Beilis endeared himself to many of the Russian drivers, who called him *nash Mendel*—our Mendel—and had nothing but good to say about him at the trial. Even the local members of the anti-Semitic Union of the Russian People displayed a respectful attitude toward Beilis, presumably because he was on friendly terms with the parish priest, a member of the Union who bought bricks from him at discount prices for a parochial school. During the pogrom of 1905, the priest and other members of the Union had come to assure Beilis that he and his family would not be harmed, nor were they. Beilis did not aspire to be a martyr. He wanted to be left alone. Throughout his long incarceration and trial—he was in prison two years and two months preceding the trial—he complained but did not grovel.

The Conspirators

What follows is a factual, unadorned account of the Beilis trial and the people who figured in its day-to-day proceedings. However, that is not the full story of the Beilis case.

The rest of the story unfolded beyond the courtroom, in the chambers of the Minister of Justice, Shcheglovitov, an official who had the ear of the czar and who used his unbridled power of the judiciary and his intimate connections with the Union of the Russian People and their representatives in the Duma to make sure that the blood-libel calumny against the Jews was fully vindicated in the Beilis trial. Working closely with Zamislovski, an influential monarchist member of the Duma who was enlisted as one of the two civil prosecutors of Beilis, Shcheglovitov moved inexorably to shape the course and set the direction of the Beilis trial. The task of relaying his concerns and instructions to the Kiev officialdom was entrusted to two loyal and like-minded henchmen—S. P. Beletsky, the director of the Department of Police, and Chaplinsky, prosecutor of the Kiev appellate court. Upon the recommendation of the governor of Kiev, Feodor Boldyrev, president of the superior court in the provincial city of Uman, who—according to the governor—"was a person of quite a definite Right orientation,"[1] was picked to preside over the trial. To make sure Boldyrev understood what was expected of him, he was immediately promoted to president of the Kiev superior court and was assured that, after the trial, he would be elevated to the exalted position of president (chief justice) of the Kiev supreme appellate court. Boldyrev did not disappoint his benefactors.

---

1. Alexander B. Tager, *The Decay of Czarism*—The Beilis Trial (Philadelphia: Jewish Publication Society, 1966), p. 170.

Throughout the trial, he persistently badgered the defense witnesses and ruled consistently in favor of the prosecution on points of order. In his summation, Boldyrev displayed an unmistakable bias against the defense. As prosecutor, the Department of Justice team picked Vipper, a conceited, snobbish official who never ceased flaunting his German origin and his anti-Semitic bias.

To prove a religiously motivated murder, a medical autopsy on the victim had to show that the method used in the murder was meant to inflict extreme pain and that it was geared to "producing" the maximum volume of blood. The initial autopsy on Yushchinsky, however, could not conclusively validate the supposed ritual-murder charge. Undismayed, the government "manipulators" invited a forensic expert from St. Petersburg to reassess the autopsy findings. Kosorotov, professor of forensic medicine at St. Petersburg University, diagnosed that "while the condition of the injuries did not warrant the conclusion that the chief purpose was the infliction of pain, the injuries were inflicted with the intention of obtaining as much blood as possible for some purpose."[2] This conclusion satisfied the "conspirators," as it provided a "scientific foundation" for the main thesis of the trial. Unknown at the time was the fact that Kosorotov received 4,000 rubles plus expenses as compensation for his "crucially valuable" testimony. This information came to light in the aftermath of the October Revolution in 1917, when hitherto secret documents were declassified, and when an Extraordinary Investigating Commission appointed by the provisional government began to unravel and expose the misdeeds of the czarist administration. Archival government documents further revealed that the compensation to Professor Kosorotov was an outright bribe and that the amount of the bribe—4,000 rubles—was negotiated by civil prosecutor Zamislovski, with the proviso that it be paid in two equal installments—Zamislovksi insisted that the last installment of 2,000 rubles be paid after the trial and be made contingent upon the nature of Kosorotov's testimony.

---

2. Tager, *Decay*, p. 56.

Determined to leave nothing to chance, Minister of Justice Shcheglovitov and company next turned their attention to the composition of the jury. Forewarned in an article in the promonarchist newspaper, *Zemshchina*, that the outcome of the trial would depend chiefly upon the personnel of the jury, court officials were instructed that persons otherwise eligible who "belonged to that element of the city population, which is most opposed to the government, should not be included in the lists of candidates for jury service."[3] To still further tighten the screws on jury selection, orders were issued "to establish a most systematic, careful and efficient surveillance over the whole personnel of the jury in the Beilis case."[4] Subsequently, an official of the Kiev police advised his superiors that "Prosecutor Vipper succeeded in eliminating the intelligentsia from the jury personnel."[5] As finally constituted, of the twelve jurors selected to decide Beilis's fate, seven turned out to be members of the notorious Union of the Russian People.

Sergei Machalin, a young revolutionary who had had several brushes with the law, viewed the anti-Jewish agitation in connection with the Yushchinsky murder as an officially inspired scheme designed to deflect the attention of the masses from the corrupt and oppressive policies of the czarist regime. Always ready to join in the fray against the government, Machalin sought out journalist Brazul and offered to assist in the Yushchinsky investigation. Having been briefed by Brazul about the possible involvement in the crime of Vera Cheberyak and her criminal cohorts, Machalin decided that his friend and fellow revolutinary, Amzor Karayev, would be ideally suited to ferret out the truth from members of the underworld. A fearless young man with an explosive temperament, Karayev's daring exploits within the revolutionary movement had earned him the reputation of a folk hero. Machalin promptly summoned Karayev to come to Kiev, and the latter obliged.

---

3. Tager, *Decay*, p. 175.
4. Ibid., p. 176.
5. Ibid., p. 177.

Government manipulators now sought to "neutralize" possible defense witness Amzor Karayev, who was considered too dangerous for the prosecution. Soon after Karayev and Sergei Machalin managed to extract a confession from Piotr Singayevsky, a half-brother of Vera Cheberyak, the government sent Karayev to Siberia for "administrative detention." The defense summoned Karayev to testify at the trial, but the government prevented his appearance "for security reasons."

A unique, indeed pivotal, role in the Beilis trial was played by a 19-year-old student of Kiev University, Vladimir Golubev. A leader of the "Double-Headed Eagle," a protégé of prosecutor Zamislovski, with connections to the highest echelons of the Union of the Russian People, Golubev's influence within all levels of the government administration in Kiev was enormous. He took a personal interest in the Beilis case from the outset, consistently shadowing and intimidating the investigators and prodding them to steer the investigation in the direction of the Jews. It was Golubev who was chiefly responsible for the removal of the investigators Mishchuk and Krasovsky from their posts for treating his theories about Beilis's guilt as "nonsense."

The provisional government's post-revolution investigating commission brought to light the depravity and judicial corruption rampant in the Justice Department under the minister of justice, Shcheglovitov. Even prior to the revolution, the minister of justice had been the target of mounting criticism by members of the bar and the liberal members of the Duma for playing havoc with Russia's judicial system. Indeed, "Shcheglovitov Justice" has become synonymous with injustice.

The minister's contempt for Jews was clearly reflected in his testimony before the commission: "It was my opinion," he asserted, "that in view of their religious peculiarities the Jews were not fit for judicial work."[6] When questioned about his abuse of judicial

---

6. Maurice Samuel, *Blood Accusation—The Strange History of the Beilis Case* (Philadelphia: Jewish Publication Society, 1966), p. 119.

power in the Beilis case, he replied: "I don't know what to say." Shcheglovitov's *mea culpa* before the commission revealed his "guiding principle" in the administration of justice: it was the czar's animosity against the Jews that determined his action, especially in the Beilis case. Stepan Beletsky, the police director who religiously followed the minister's orders in subverting judicial procedures in the Beilis case, broke down before the commission, mumbling, "I blush for myself. . . . I am glad to confess . . . I have a little girl of fifteen and a son; his schoolmates may tell them about this."[7]

With regard to the bribe offered to Kosorotov, professor of forensic medicine at St. Petersburg University, which was handled by Beletsky on behalf of Shcheglovitov, Beletsky testified: "I began my conversation with Kosorotov very carefully . . . the professor, however, took it quite calmly and demanded 4,000 rubles." Professor Kosorotov fulfilled his assignment at the trial to the satisfaction of the minister of justice, but he was foolish enough to give receipts, which were produced before the commission. With regard to the chain of command on the Beilis case, Beletsky was explicit: "It led from Golubev to Chaplinsky to Zamislovski to Shcheglovitov; the idea of a ritual murder began with Golubev and Chaplinsky."[8]

Posted at the trial were two government agents who reported daily to Beletsky, primarily on the "correctness" of the presiding judge's conduct. They pointed out, inter alia, that "Cheberyak had probably poisoned her own children" and that "all the luminaries of law, literature, medicine and science are on the side of Jewry . . . against them stands the soul of the simple people (the jury), who will pronounce their incorruptible verdict . . . and this will be God's judgment on the Jews."[9]

The pervasive influence exerted by the Union of the Russian People and its local surrogate, the Double-Headed Eagle, upon

---

7. Ibid., p. 123.
8. Ibid., p. 172.
9. Samuel, *Blood Accusation*, p. 173.

some of the investigators surfaced in the course of the commission's later inquiries. Evidence available to the commission revealed that two detectives, Polishchuk and Vygranov, who had initially worked as trusted aids of Krasovsky, had received compensation from a slush fund maintained by the above-mentioned monarchist organizations and had transmitted confidential information to their leaders.

It was also disclosed that Colonel Pavel Ivanove, head of the Kiev gendarmery, who was called to testify at the trial as a defense witness, had apparently succumbed to official pressure and concealed information favorable to the defense. What Colonel Ivanove failed to disclose at the trial was the fact that it was he who was pressured by his superiors to "plant" the police informer Kazachenko in Beilis's cell in order to manufacture evidence against Beilis. Kazachenko testified before the magistrate that Beilis had tried to hire him to poison two witnesses and that he would be generously rewarded for his efforts. Kazachenko had subsequently confessed to Colonel Ivanove that he had invented the story to ingratiate himself with the authorities, but when questioned at the trial, the colonel had a memory lapse. What Colonel Ivanove deigned to remember—without corroboration—was that "all the parties in private investigation received remuneration," and he named Brazul-Brushkovsky, Sergei Machalin, and Amzor Karayev, witnesses for the defense. When challenged by defense lawyer Gruzenberg to reveal the source of his information, Colonel Ivanove pleaded "official secrecy" and was upheld by the presiding judge. Prosecutor Zamislovski reminded Gruzenberg derisively that Colonel Ivanove was invited to testify at the behest of the defense, whereupon Gruzenberg shot back, "It doesn't matter who invited him. There are no witnesses for the prosecution or for the defense. There are only honest and dishonest witnesses." This evoked a sharp reprimand from the presiding judge: "I must warn you . . . that I shall be compelled to take extreme measures."[10]

---

10. Samuel, *Blood Accusation*, p. 209.

The Religious Expertise

Throughout the trial, the presiding judge, Boldyrev, kept reminding the defense lawyers—in a lackadaisical manner—that Judaism and the Jewish religion were not on trial in this case, merely individual Jews belonging to "fanatical sects." Yet the religious experts summoned to testify at the trial were permitted to roam over all aspects of Judaism.

Strangely enough, the prosecution could not find even one authoritative church scholar of the Greek Orthodox faith—the official religion of the Russian empire—to testify as an expert in support of the "ritual murder" practice of the Jews, as alleged by the prosecution. Instead, justice minister Shcheglovitov and his associates dredged up an obscure Catholic priest residing in far-off Tashkent, Turkestan, to act as the star religious expert for the prosecution. The priest, Justin Pranaitis, while living in St. Petersburg, wrote a pamphlet in 1893, *The Christians in the Jewish Talmud*, or *The Secrets of the Teachings of the Rabbis about Christians*, to prove that the practice of ritual murder is countenanced by the Jewish religion. He brought the pamphlet to the attention of the Congress of the United Nobility, a conglomerate of titled estate owners aligned with the Union of the Russian People, but he did not receive the acclaim and reward he had hoped for. Subsequently, he tried his hand at extortion, failing which, he betook himself to Tashkent. In Tashkent he ran afoul of the Greek Orthodox church for trying to convert Russians to Catholicism, which prompted the ministry of the interior to instruct the local authorities "to inflict upon the priest Pranaitis the appropriate penalty" for a "tactless display of Catholic fanaticism toward the Greek-Orthodox church."[11] The priest's dubious credentials notwithstanding, Prosecutor Vipper declared that "no one so learned, courageous and steadfast was to be found among the Greek-Orthodox clergy." Pranaitis's striking, imposing appear-

---

11. Tager, *Decay*, p. 201.

ance and his vitriolic diatribe against the Jews seem to have made a strong impression upon the benighted jury and caused uneasiness and concern among Beilis's defenders. Pitted against Pranaitis, however, were three eminent scholars, Professors Troyitsky and Kovovtsev representing Russia's foremost academies of higher learning, and the highly esteemed and erudite Moscow rabbi, Jacob Mazeh. As Pranaitis continued to drone on for two days, flaying Jewish practices and beliefs, his persuasive power gradually diminished, especially after he was subjected to a vigorous cross-examination by the defense. Consequently, agents of the department of police wired their superiors in St. Petersburg that "the cross-examination of Pranaitis reduced the power of his arguments and disclosed a lack of knowledge of the texts."

Another internal message to St. Petersburg indicated that "Professors Troyitsky and Kovovtsev, who testified after Pranaitis, offered conclusions favorable to the defense, praising the dogmas of the Jewish religion ruling out the possibility that Jews commit religious murders."

In spite of Pranaitis's lackluster performance, the Beilis defense team was not persuaded that the priest's testimony had been decisively discredited in the eyes of the jury.

Thus, to further expose Pranaitis's ignorance in terms intelligible to the simple, untutored peasants of the jury, the defense decided to resort to an ingenious ploy to test the priest's knowledge by asking him to explain certain Aramaic titles of Talmudic lore. At the following session of the court, one of the defense lawyers asked Pranaitis to explain the meaning of the word *Hullin*, a tractate dealing with preparation of animal food.

The priest replied: "I don't know."

"What is the meaning of the word *Eruvin*?" (Walking limits on the Sabbath.)

Pranaitis: "I don't know."

"What is the meaning of the word *Yevamot*?" (Dealing with laws of marriage.)

Pranaitis: "I don't know."

"When did Baba Bathra live, and what was her activity?"

Pranaitis: "I don't know."

The last question elicited a burst of laughter from the audience, which was partly Jewish. The reason was simple: *Baba Bathra* is not a person, but a talmudic tractate meaning "The Lower Gate" and dealing with property laws. However, *Baba* in Russian refers to a peasant woman, which obviously led the priest astray.

The cumulative effect of these unanswered questions was devastating for Pranaitis and the prosecution.[12]

---

12. Samuel, *Blood Accusation*, p. 215.

2

The Beilis Trial

First day of the trial: September 25, 1913
   Presiding judge: F. A. Boldyrev
   Prosecutor: O. V. Vipper
   Civil prosecutors: S. Shmakov, G. G. Zamislovski
   For the defense: O. O. Gruzenberg, N. B. Karabchevsky, D. N.
Grigorevich-Barsky, A. S. Zarudny, V. A. Maklakov
   Presiding judge to defendant Beilis:

   Q. Do you belong to the lower middle class?
   A. Yes.
   Q. How old are you?
   A. Thirty-nine.
   Q. Are you a permanent resident of Kiev?
   A. Yes.
   Q. Are you a Jew?
   A. Yes, a Jew.
   Q. Are you literate?

A. Yes.
Q. Married?
A. Yes, yes.
Q. You have children?
A. Yes, five.
Q. Your profession?
A. Clerk.
Q. You possess property?
A. No.

Preface

As a courtroom drama, the Beilis case does not conform to a conventional "whodunit" scenario.

The scenario for the central plot—the murder of a 13-year-old Christian boy, Andrey Yushchinsky, and the indictment of a 39-year-old Jew, Mendel Beilis, as the alleged murderer—appears to have been written by two different scriptwriters with disparate objectives in mind. One script, objective and straightforward, focused on identifying and apprehending the murderer, while the other, the politicized script, centered on validating a myth that the Jewish religion prescribed the use of Christian blood for ritual purposes. Accordingly, the lead players, hewing to two conflicting scripts, found themselves at loggerheads in acting out their specific roles. From the very outset, the Kiev investigators—Mishchuk, Fenenko, Kirichenko, and Krasovsky—operating on the premise that this was an ordinary murder, committed by ordinary criminals, were on a collision course with Beletsky, Chaplinsky, Golubev, and others, who followed the politicized script—a script laced with high-level government intrigue and judicial corruption. The mastermind of this officially inspired script was the minister of justice, I. G. Shcheglovitov. The Kiev investigators built up a solid case against

Vera Cheberyak and her criminal associates—Rudzinsky, Latyshev, and Singayevsky—the perpetrators of the crime, while Shcheglovitov's underlings, using the immense power and resources of the government, were hell-bent to convict a Jew, Mendel Beilis, of murdering Yushchinsky for religious ritual purposes.

Synopsis of the Official Indictment

The long, tortuous formal indictment may be summarized as follows:

The corpse of 13-year-old Andrey Yuschinsky was discovered in a cave on the outskirts of Kiev on March 20, 1911. He was the illegitimate son of Alexandra Prihodko, the wife of Luka Prihodko, a bookbinder. Andrey left home for school on March 12, did not appear at school, and never returned home. It was established that the boy had been murdered elsewhere, by more than one person, and was brought to the cave after his death. It was also ascertained that Yushchinsky played truant on March 12 and instead of going to school, went to visit his friend Zhenya, son of Vassily and Vera Cheberyak, whose home was a known hangout for Kiev's underworld. At the murdered boy's funeral, leaflets were distributed by a member of the Union of the Russian People, a rabidly anti-Semitic monarchist organization, accusing Jews of killing the boy for religious purposes and exhorting the populace to avenge the blood of the "martyred" youth. A preliminary investigation led the authorities to suspect relatives of Yushchinsky in the crime, but as the evidence against them proved baseless, attention was focused on the criminal coterie clustered around Vera Cheberyak.

Enter Brazul-Brushkovsky (herein referred to as "Brazul")

A journalist, Brazul began a private investigation of the murder, motivated by idealistic reasons as well as a desire for self-promotion.

Brazul-Brushkovsky, a Russian with a Jewish wife—a fact which, in Prosecutor Vipper's mind, disqualified him as a full-fledged Russian—was an idealistic, ambitious journalist who was genuinely determined to expose the ritual-murder accusation against the Jews as a fabrication. In his yearlong investigative activities, he also sought to prove his mettle as an ingenious investigative reporter worthy of national recognition. The prosecution repeatedly portrayed him as a "meddlesome, amateur sleuth" whose real aim was to mislead the investigating authorities.

Brazul proceeded to cultivate Vera Cheberyak on the assumption that while she may not have been personally involved in the crime, her underworld connections might prove useful in identifying the real culprits. He wined and dined her for a period of six months, greased her palm with occasional gifts, and became a frequent visitor in her home. In his naïveté, he trusted her completely in spite of the warnings of his colleagues that she seemed to be a pathological liar. He thus swallowed her yarn that her erstwhile French lover, Miffle, whom she had blinded in a fit of jealous rage, was one of the murderers of Yushchinsky. Beguiled by her wiles, Brazul arranged and paid for a trip to Kharkov when she told him that she had to obtain valuable information from one of her underworld friends who was serving time in Kharkov. To confound matters, Brazul persuaded his friend Arnold Margolin, who was then Beilis's attorney, to meet Cheberyak in Kharkov so as to be privy to the "valuable information" she was prepared to impart. As a result of that meeting, Margolin was subsequently barred from representing Beilis; instead, he was summoned as a witness in the case. It finally dawned on Brazul that Cheberyak had played him for a fool and that the woman he had trusted so implicitly was, in fact, an accessory to the crime. In May, Brazul began publishing a series of articles in *Kievskaya Mysil*, in which he named Cheberyak, as well as Rudzinsky, Latyshev, and Singayevsky as the murderers of Yushchinsky. Thus, Brazul-Brushkovsky's role in the Beilis case was that of a well-meaning investigator who, because of his gullibility and naïveté, was not equal to the task he set for himself. It must be said, to his credit, that he did cooperate with the investigators Krasovsky, Karayev, and Machalin in setting up the crucial meeting with Singayevsky, at which the latter blurted out a full confession.

In her first deposition before the magistrate, Vera Cheberyak referred to Luka Prihodko (Yushchinsky's stepfather), Nezhinsky (a relative), and Miffle (her erstwhile French paramour) as having had a hand in the crime. She described her trip to Kharkov with Brazul and Vygranov, a former police detective, to meet A. D. Margolin, Beilis's first lawyer, who—according to Cheberyak—had asked her to take responsibility for the murder, promising her 40,000 rubles for this "service". Brazul, Margolin, and Vygranov emphatically denied that such an offer was ever made.

The Minister of Justice Takes a Hand

At the same time, two anti-Semitic organizations, the Union of the Russian People and its local surrogate, The Double-Headed Eagle, acting through Vladimir Golubev, continued their agitation designed to pin the blame for the Yushchinsky murder upon Jews, stressing the multiple wounds inflicted on the boy as symptomatic of a ritual murder. To give the case national notoriety, they enlisted the assistance of G. G. Zamislovski, a prominent monarchist member of the Imperial Duma who was soon to become one of the civil prosecutors at the Beilis trial and, through him, Minister of Justice Shcheglovitov. A protégé of the czar, Shcheglovitov decided to put the full resources of his department at the disposal of the Union of the Russian People and the local officials answerable to him, with the aim of making the ritual-murder accusation against Jews the centerpiece of what was soon to evolve into the Beilis trial. To give the accusation a semblance of "scientific respectability," experts were summoned to assess the psychological and religious aspects of the crime.

Enter the Experts

Sikorsky, professor emeritus of psychology at Kiev University, and Father Justin Pranaitis, a defrocked Catholic priest, testified that the Yushchsinky murder represented a classic example of a ritual murder committed in conformity with Judaic law as interpreted by the sages and savants of Judaism. Professors Glagolev, Troyitsky, and Kovovtsev, representing Russia's foremost academic institutions, and Rabbi Jacob Mazeh, the erudite Moscow rabbi, repudiated the testimonies of Sikorsky and Pranaitis, asserting that the spilling of human blood is repugnant to Judaism and contrary to its teachings (see "Religious Expertise" and Gruzenberg's summation).

The "Evidence" against Beilis

Testimony to the effect that a "black-bearded" man had chased children playing on the grounds of the Zaitsev brick factory, seizing Andrey and dragging him toward the factory kiln, was provided by Vera and Vassily Cheberyak, based on what Zhenya, their son, had told them prior to his demise (from an attack of dysentery). This and the rambling testimony of Kazimir and Yuliana Shachovsky, which was based on what a derelict "wolf woman" had told them, represented the sum total of the evidence against Beilis. Zhenya Cheberyak was obviously unavailable to substantiate the Cheberyaks' testimony. Furthermore, the Shachovskys subsequently repudiated their disclosures, explaining that detectives Polishchuk and Vygranov, plying them with vodka, had warned them to implicate Beilis. It was on the basis of this uncorroborated hearsay evidence that Beilis was handpicked by Golubev as the defendant in this case.

The Indictment: An Official Transcript

On March 20, 1911, within the City of Kiev on the estate of Berner, some distance from any built-up areas, in one of the many caves to be found there, within 150 feet from Nagorskaya Street was found the body of a boy in a sitting position, hands tied behind his back, wearing a shirt, underpants and one sock. Within the cave some distance from the body lay a second sock of the same color and looks as the one worn, also a cap and jacket, a leather belt and under his head stuffed into a crevice in the wall were five folded copybooks bearing the inscription "student, Andrey Yushchinsky"; stamped on one of the copybooks was the imprint "Kiev-Sophist Religious School." The head and body bore a variety of wounds, but traces of blood in the cave were not observed. The identity of the deceased was soon established to be that of 13-year-old Andrey Yushchinsky, the son out of wedlock of Alexandra Prihodko and a student in the preparatory class of the Kiev-Sophist Religious School. A court-initiated medical examination and autopsy revealed numerous wounds caused by a sharp object on the head and body. The examiners were in agreement that the wounds were inflicted by more than one person, at least two, but more likely several. A preliminary investigation established the following facts:

For several years prior to May 1910, Yushchinsky lived with his mother and stepfather, Luka Prihodko, in Kiev in the section of the City known as Lukyanovka, which also is the site of the Berner estate. Thereafter, he moved with them to Slobodka, a suburb of the City of Kiev. Joining them in this move were his grandmother and aunt, Olimpiada Nezhinsky and Natalia Yushchinsky, whom he visited almost daily. In August, thanks to the efforts of his aunt, Yushchinsky was placed in the Kiev-Sophist Religious School which he attended from Slobodka, leaving very early in the morning. While living in Slobodka, Yushchinsky occasionally ventured into Lukyanovka to see and play with his former friends, of whom he was especially friendly with Zhenya Cheberyak. On the 12th of March, rising as usual very early, Yushchinsky breakfasted on borscht left over from yesterday's dinner and taking his books and copybooks left home around 6:00 A.M. on the way to Kiev. While still in Slobodka he was seen at one place by Pavel Pushka and at another place when he was approaching the bridge over the Dnieper River he was seen by Maria Pushka. However, on that day he did not appear at school, nor did he return home. Assuming at first that he went to spend the night with Natalia Yushchinsky, which he was wont to do quite frequently, his mother was not particularly worried by his absence, but on the morning of the following day when it was revealed that he was not at his aunt's, Alexandra Prihodko began looking for him among relatives and acquaintances whom he might have visited. Taking all possible measures in the search, she notified the police and the school's administration of her son's disappearance and also together with her husband visited the offices of the Kiev-based newspaper *Kievskaya Mysel*, asking that a notice be printed about her son's disappearance. Her search over the next several days was equally in vain until the body of Andrey Yushchinsky was finally discovered. An autopsy showed the stomach containing chunks of potatoes and beets, apparently remnants of the borscht which had not yet been digested. This circumstance revealed, according to the doctors, that Yushchinsky died within 3 to 4 hours after he had eaten.

When the preliminary investigation was about to begin, just prior to interviewing the witnesses, there appeared before the magistrate without a summons on March 22 a staff member of the above newspaper *Kievskaya Mysel*, the Jew Barschevsky, who related about the visit to the newspaper of the mother of Yushchinsky. He said his attention was drawn by her strange behavior. According to him, the mother, while reporting the disappearance of her son, did not appear distraught and did not show any signs of grief about the loss of her son; she was composed and, in fact, smiled as did the man with her when asked to which address should information about her son be forwarded. Barschevsky's declaration about Alexandra

Prihodko's indifference to her son's disappearance was subsequently contradicted by other people who stated that Alexandra Prihodko, when recounting the extensive search for her lost son, was crying and seemed very dejected. The preliminary investigation focused on Barschevsky's statement and suspicions. On orders from the Commandant of the Kiev Police Detective Division, Mishchuk, Alexandra and Luka Prihodko were arrested on the 24th of March and on the 25th and 26th of March their apartment was searched by detectives of the Kiev Police. From the walls the detectives removed seven pieces of plaster bearing dark brown spots; also taken were Alexandra's skirt and blouse, a work shirt of Luka, and two rags. Nevertheless no evidence against the Prihodkos was secured and on April 5, they were released. A chemical microscopic analysis of the items taken revealed no traces of blood.

At the same time rumors gained currency in Kiev that Yushchinsky was killed by Jews for religious reasons. Yet, the involvement of his mother and stepfather in his death persisted and shaped the course of the investigation. Apart from the version attributing the death of the boy to his mother and relatives, another version had been gaining credence. The boy's murder was now being ascribed to criminal elements, several of whom had sought to get rid of the boy who allegedly had knowledge of their criminal activity and thus posed a threat of exposing specific criminal acts perpetrated by them. As a participant in the murder the name of the mother of the aforementioned Zhenya Cheberyak, Vera Cheberyak, was mentioned, the latter having close contacts and association with the underworld. However, no solid evidence having been adduced in support of the last version, other developments in the case led to the conclusion that the Jew, Mendel Beilis, was involved in the crime for religious motives, in consequence of which Beilis was arrested as a defendant in the case. Immediately thereafter the version linking the crime to the underworld, which had surfaced previously, had arisen in a modified form. According to the new version, the murder was committed by criminal elements in order to pin the blame on Jews and thus provoke a pogrom. A pogrom in turn would offer the criminals an opportunity to profit from the plunder resulting therefrom. This version ruled out the participation of Vera Cheberyak in the murder. The interrogation of Beilis and his incarceration took place on August 3, 1911, and on the 25th of the month the investigating magistrate was provided with substantive proof confirming the latest version concerning the murder.

The preliminary investigation in the Yushchinsky case was completed on January 5, 1912, and the indictment was drafted on January 10th. On the 18th of January, the Prosecutor of the Kiev District Court received a statement pertaining to the case from a staff member of the newspaper *Russkoye Slovo*, Brazul-Brushkovsky, who also served on the staff of the aforementioned newspaper *Kievskaya Mysel*. In this statement, the above-mentioned Brazul-Brushkovsky revealed that he had been following the case since its inception and had come to the conclusion that Yushchinsky's murder was the work of a gang of criminals, much of whose activities was well known to Yushchinsky; this impelled them to kill the boy, who posed a constant threat to their safety. Thus, in order to cover up their tracks and mislead the investigating authorities, they sought to cook up a ritualistic murder. The above statement had no impact upon the course of the Beilis case and the disclosures embodied therein were not turned over to the authorities for a further investigation. The case was scheduled for a hearing on May 17, 1912. On May 6th the officer in charge of the investigation, Commander of the Kiev Gendazmezy, Col. Ivanove, received from Brazul-Brushkovsky a new announcement in which the above named repeated his contention that Yushchinsky was killed by persons belonging to a gang of professional thieves, naming three: Singayevsky, Rudzinsky, and Latyshev. The announcement said that the murder was committed with the knowledge of Vera Cheberyak and in her apartment and that the multiple injuries to the boy were explainable by the fact that he was tortured in order to extract a confession as to what he told the police authorities about the gang's crimes. The newspaperman further stated that the stabs on the boy's body were made by an awl, the murder weapon being especially adaptable to keep the flow of blood to a minimum and to avoid leaving traces of the crime. Nevertheless, blood spots remained on the floor, wall, and carpet of the Cheberyak flat. In confirmation of the above, Brazul-Brushkovsky referred to relevant testimony of one Mrs. Malitsky, and he was also prepared to provide two witnesses who accidentally walked into the Cheberyak flat right after the murder, plus two additional witnesses in whom Singayevsky had confidence and to whom he practically confessed his part in the murder. At a subsequently held inquest, Brazul-Brushkovsky pointed out the witnesses, indicating that the sisters Dyakonov entered the Cheberyak flat after the murder, while the confession by Singayevsky was made to Karayev in the presence of Machalin. In view of the newly offered data, the Yushchinsky case was referred for further investigation, revealing the following circumstances.

The evidence in the case was collected by Brazul-Brushkovsky in cooperation with Vygranov, Krasovsky, Machalin, and Karayev. Krasovsky at one time supervised the Kiev Detective Division and subsequently became its Commander. When the head of the Kiev Detective Division, Mishchuk, was relieved of his duties in connection with the Yushchinsky investigation, the task was assigned to Col. Ivanove with Krasovsky, a police officer who led the investigation from May to September, 1911, as his assistant. Soon thereafter he, too, was relieved of this assignment and returned to his original place of service; in January of 1912 he was dismissed from the police department. While Krasovsky was engaged in the Yushchinsky investigation as a police officer, one of his assistants was Vygranov, a former agent of the detective division, who was subsequently dismissed by Krasovsky himself. According to Brazul-Brushkovsky, Vygranov started working for him in August or September, 1911. Working jointly they secured the information embodied in his first statement to the authorities, which by his own admission, he did not believe to be true. In April, 1912, Krasovksy proposed that they work jointly and in February of that year he was approached with a proposal to be of service by a student who took courses in farm management, by the name of Machalin, who in turn invited his acquaintance, Karayev, to join them in order to accelerate the investigation. The latter, namely Karayev, having spent three and a half years in the Kiev prison for a crime against the government, was familiar with the criminal world. Krasovsky explained that Karayev's readiness to take part in the investigation was motivated by his desire "to rehabilitate himself" in the eyes of society as well as in the eyes of his like-minded associates, who suspected him of being an agent provocateur. Brazul-Brushkovsky and his co-workers, proceeding on the premise that the Cheberyak woman was implicated in the murder of Yushchinsky, decided to try to get information from persons close to her. With this in mind, Krasovsky and Vygranov struck up an acquaintanceship with the sisters Dyakonov, who frequented the Cheberyak home, while Karayev assumed the task of gaining the trust of Cheberyak's brother, Singayevsky. Krasovsky testified that in chatting with the Dyakonov sisters he found out from Katherine Dyakonov that on March 11th, in her presence, Yushchinsky walked into the Cheberyak home and engaged Zhenya Cheberyak in conversation about gunpowder. The next day, around 12:00 noon, she again walked over to the Cheberyak home, and while entering the anteroom, she saw Latyshev, Singayevsky, and Rudzinsky rushing out from one room to another. At the same time, she noticed that the carpet usually spread out in that room was rolled up in the form of a tube and was shoved under the sofa. At one time, Katherine Dyakonov told Krasovsky that when the killing of Yushchinsky began and the boy started screaming, Vera Cheberyak ordered her associates to rip off a pillowcase and stuff it into the boy's mouth; another time she reported that Yushchinsky was stabbed with a stiletto to avoid spattering the blood, and while one participant was doing the stabbing, the other wiped off the blood with a rag. When questioned as to the source of this information Katherine Dyakonov answered Krasovsky that it was Vera Cheberyak herself who told her about it "out of friendship." Karayev deposed that striking up an acquaintanceship with Singayevsky, he sought to steer the conversation toward the Yushchinsky murder. At one of these conversations, Singayevsky said that the Yushchinsky case was being pinned on him, Latyshev, and Rudzinsky and "Verka" Cheberyak, in whose flat the boy was killed. In an attempt to elicit a confession, Karayev told Singayevsky that he had reliable information that the arrest of Vera Cheberyak and Singayevsky was imminent. This unnerved Singayevsky, and he revealed his intention to kill without delay the Dyakonov sisters, who he said "are tattling to the authorities." Karayev proposed that in consultation with Machalin, who in the meantime had also met Singayevsky, they should assess the situation and take such steps as may be necessary to avert the threat of arrest. In Machalin's presence he, Karayev, said, pointing to Singayevsky: "Here is the real murderer of Yushchinsky, who in concert with Vera Cheberyak, Rudzinsky, and Latyshev participated in the murder." He then asked Singayevsky if that's the way it was, and the latter answered: "Yes, this was our job." At Machalin's suggestion that he reveal the details, Singayevsky said that on the morning of March 12th, "they took care of business," after which they departed for Moscow, and in response to the question why they did such a "dirty job," leaving "footprints," he replied, "It was the 'ministerial head' of Rudzinsky that planned it that way." Machalin, confirming Karayev's deposition, added that Singayevsky, in confessing to the murder of Yushchinsky, revealed that the murder was committed by him, Rudzinsky, and Latyshev in Vera Cheberyak's flat and that soon thereafter the Dyakonov sisters walked in; however, they managed to sneak out to the next room, throwing a coat over the corpse so that the sisters saw neither them nor the corpse. Katherine Dyakonov declared at her hearing that she had frequently visited Vera Cheberyak. On March 11th at about 12:00 noon she paid another visit and between 12:00 and 1:00 P.M. Yushchinsky came to see Zhenya Cheberyak about the gunpowder. The boys planned to go for a walk, but when she left the flat around 3:00 P.M., Yushchinsky was still there. The following day after 12:00 noon Katherine again visited Vera Cheberyak. Entering the foyer, she saw in one of the rooms four persons, namely, Singayevsky,

Latyshev, Rudzinsky, as well as Lysunov, who—when noticing her—
fled into another room. The rug in the room was folded halfway, but
its appearance did not suggest to her that it covered up some object.
Consequently, she dreamt that the body of Yushchinsky was inside
the rug. As previously indicated, Katherine Dyakonov deposed that
on March 11, Yushchinsky visited the Cheberyak flat between 12:00
and 1:00 P.M. and remained there when Katherine left around 3:00
P.M. In the interim, it was established that on that day Yushchinsky
was in school until the end of classes at 12 noon, after which he and
a classmate took a walk not on Lukyanovka, where the Cheberyaks
lived, but on Vladimir Street, taking leave of his classmate near the
city theatre. On instructions from his aunt, Natalie Yushchinsky,
who owned a workshop for making boxes, Andrey was to buy
special thumbtacks at the Bessarabian Bazaar, where he apparently
went directly after school, coming home with the thumbtacks
around 3:00 P.M. Katherine Dyakonov's assertion that on March 12
she saw at the Cheberyak flat four persons was contradicted by the
statements made by Krasovsky and Vygranov, whom she had told
that she saw only three—Singayevsky, Latyshev, and Rudzinsky, as
well as her own testimony before Colonel Ivanove when she had
referred to only three persons, never mentioning Lysunov. Apart
from that, information gathered in the course of the investigation
revealed that from February 28 to March 17, 1911, Lysunov was in
prison. Ksenia Dyakonov, diverging from Katherine's version of
what transpired, stated that her sister had never told her anything
about Yushchinsky's murder and that there was never a conversation between them as to who could have done him in. Indeed,
Colonel Ivanove gained the impression that Katherine's conflicting
testimony was the result of "tutoring" by someone else. The testimony of Mrs. Malitsky, referred to in the statement by Brazul-
Brushkovsky, can be summarized as follows: On the 23rd of November, 1911, at the hearing before a magistrate, she stated that during
the month of March, 1911, not long before the body of Yushchinsky
was discovered, she was staying in her apartment situated just

below the Cheberyak flat and heard around 11 o'clock in the morning the sound of steps, which she had assumed to be those of Vera Cheberyak. Thereafter, it sounded as if a child was running and then from the same direction she heard the steps of two adults. Then she heard a child's cry, a scream, and finally some commotion. The same day somewhat later, she found out from some women that the Cheberyak children were not at home at that time. Some days thereafter, she had heard children talking among themselves that blood-spattered rags were strewn all over the garbage hole but she had not seen the rags herself. At a subsequent hearing, in December of the same year, Mrs. Malitsky added that some time after she had heard a child's screams emanating from the Cheberyak flat, she had clearly heard several people carrying a heavy object, which they deposited on the floor and dragged through the room. At that point, there was a disapproving outcry from Vera Cheberyak. At subsequent hearings there were significant variations in the story. When questioned by a friend as to why she had withheld the information for so long, Mrs. Malitsky replied that she would have kept her mouth shut if Vera Cheberyak had not insulted her, but now she would have her revenge. In November of that year, District Supervisor Kirichenko, in looking over the flat in which Cheberyak resided in March, noticed on the wallpaper dark spots resembling blood spots. To verify the above and also the testimony of Mrs. Malitsky concerning the blood-spattered rags in the garbage hole, the Court Supervisor initiated the same month an examination of the garbage hole in the presence of a court physician and removed for inspection seven pieces of plaster from the walls of the Cheberyak flat containing the suspicious spots. The blood-spattered rags in the garbage hole have not been found and the spots on the plaster pieces were on examination found devoid of blood. Also, the Cheberyak rug referred to in Brazul-Brushkovsky's testimony was, upon a thorough chemical-microscopic examination, found to be free of blood.

Testimony of Vera Cheberyak

Questioned by a magistrate about Brazul-Brushkovsky's allegations, Vera Cheberyak testified that Brazul, becoming acquainted with her through Vygranov, started frequenting her home, asking her to tell him all she knew about the murder of Yushchinsky and to collect evidence about the murder, a request with which she had complied. In the course of their conversations, the families of Prihodko, Nezhinsky, and Miffle were mentioned. Occasionally Brazul and Vygranov raised the question whether she would agree to take the responsibility for the Yushchinsky murder "on herself," telling her that she could thereby make a "nice bundle." She repeatedly declined. On one such occasion when she reiterated her refusal, Brazul said, "Well, in that case let's continue what we started, let's give Miffle the axe." Brazul at that time was in possession of a draft of disclosure made out in the name of the prosecutor, pointing to Miffle and other persons as the killers of Yushchinsky. Familiarizing her with the contents of the draft, Brazul suggested that they confirm the disclosure, adding that he could "embellish" the statement as Vera desired. In a later interrogation before Colonel Ivanove, Vera admitted telling the truth only partly, having embellished "quite a bit."

Trip to Kharkov

The investigation revealed that in December, 1911, Brazul, Vygranov, and Vera Cheberyak traveled to Kharkov to meet, according to Brazul, an "important personality." The important personality turned out to be Kiev attorney Margolin, who from January 1912 had entered the case as Beilis's lawyer. According to Vera Cheberyak's deposition of December 5, Brazul forewarned her that on the following day they would take a trip, not naming the destination, for an audience with an important personality whom Brazul identified, to the best of her recollection, as a member of the Imperial Duma. Brazul told Vera that she could tell the gentleman about the dismissal of her husband from his position, as well as other troubles that she had experienced in connection with the Yush-chinsky case. She agreed, and on the following day Vygranov and Perechrist (a worker for the editorial department of *Kievskaya Mysel*) visited her and suggested that they proceed to the railway station. En route, Vygranov told Vera that they were going to Kharkov. She traveled with Vygranov and Brazul second-class on the Kharkov Express.

In Kharkov they checked in at a hotel and proceeded to the audience. They arrived at another, more ostentatious and richly furnished hotel, and in one of the rooms met a gentleman whom Brazul introduced to Vera. The gentleman asked her several questions related to the Yushchinsky case and then solicited her help in connection with the case. She asked what she could do to help, and the gentleman proposed that she take the responsibility for the murder "upon herself," promising her "big money." Just at that time, three persons appeared from behind a partition concealing the door to another room and one of them said: "Well, what do you say, Cheberyak? Take it. There is forty thousand in it for you." She declined. Then one of the persons tried to persuade her not to fear, saying that they would provide her with documents that would make her "invisible" and that she would be defended by the best lawyers. He asked her to think it over.

Vera and her traveling companions returned to their hotel and Brazul tried repeatedly to persuade her to accept the proffered offer, but she refused. The following day, they returned to Kiev. She did not share in the expenses of the trip, as Brazul took care of everything, indicating that the trip was paid for by the gentleman they traveled to meet. Brazul further indicated that that gentleman had access to "big money" from the "society," which he identified only as "our circle." He added that he personally did not have the resources to travel around and pay for others and carry on his investigation; when he needed money, he got it from the gentleman they had met.

Interrogated about the trip to Kharkov, Brazul claimed that the trip took place because Vera Cheberyak found it necessary to secure certain data about the case in that city. Earlier, wishing to test his own impression of Vera Cheberyak against that of a "fresh person," he chose attorney Margolin, who was involved in communal affairs. After some hesitation, Margolin agreed, and they decided to arrange an appointment in Kharkov to coincide with a planned business trip to Kharkov by Margolin. Not wishing to compromise Margolin as an acquaintance of Cheberyak, Brazul did not name him, except to say that he was a member of the Kharkov city council. Besides himself and Vygranov, they were joined on the trip by Perechrist, whom Brazul invited to go along to keep an eye on Cheberyak while in Kharkov. Perechrist traveled in a different compartment, unbeknownst to Cheberyak. The fact that Brazul paid for the trip did not faze him since, as a journalist, he felt he had exclusive rights to "the case."

They arrived in Kharkov in the evening and immediately the three of them proceeded to the hotel where Margolin was staying. At Brazul's suggestion, Vera Cheberyak told Margolin what she knew about the Yushchinsky case, which was a repetition of what she had previously revealed to Brazul. No one besides him and Vygranov witnessed the conversation, and Margolin did not try to persuade Cheberyak to take upon herself the responsibility for the Yushchinsky murder, nor did he promise to reward her for her efforts in the case. Thereafter, they returned to their hotel and the following morning again visited Margolin. At this short meeting Margolin never made any propositions to Cheberyak. The same day, they returned to Kiev. However, before their departure for Kiev, neither he nor Vygranov questioned Cheberyak whether she had acquired any new information while in Kharkov. They did not meet with Perechrist until their departure, but Vygranov found out from Perechrist during the train ride back to Kiev that Cheberyak did not go anywhere while in Kharkov.

Besides Margolin, Brazul also "showed" Vera Cheberyak to his newspaper colleagues in Kiev, Yablonovsky and Ordinsky, with the same purpose in mind, namely, to compare impressions. The meeting took place in a private room of a restaurant, at which time Cheberyak repeated the same details she had told Margolin in Kharkov.

Vera Cheberyak testified that at the meeting in the private room of the restaurant sometime following the Kharkov trip, she met the same three men who were present at her meeting with the "prominent gentleman" in Kharkov, who emerged from behind a partition. The same person who at that time quoted the reward figure of 40,000 rubles told her, among other things, that she ought to accept that proposal.

Vygranov and Margolin confirmed the testimony of Brazul. According to the testimonies of Brazul and Vygranov, their trip to Kharkov was prompted by a desire to obtain information pertinent to the Yushchinsky case through Vera Cheberyak, who claimed that such information was premised on her meeting with Lysunov, a prisoner in the Kharkov jail. However, they did not check in advance whether Lysunov was actually in Kharkov at the time. Information available to the investigating authorities showed that Lysunov was not in prison in Kharkov in 1911.

Reporting to Krasovsky about the Kharkov trip, Brazul explained that he deemed it imperative to share the information expected from Cheberyak with attorney Margolin who—quoting Krasovsky—as a prominent Jewish community leader in Kiev was interested in unraveling the Yushchinsky case and demolishing the allegations that it was a ritual murder.

The Experts

The special circumstances surrounding the Yushchinsky murder—the exceptionally peculiar method of the crime, along with a widespread notion that it was committed by Jews spurred by religious fanaticism—prompted the investigating authorities to invite expert opinion in order to clarify a number of questions relevant to the case with regard to the possibility that the murder was the work of mentally ill persons, and whether the data assembled offered some indication as to the aim and intentions of the murderer, his possible profession and nationality. It was decided to seek the opinion of one known for his work in the field of psychology, physician-psychiatrist and professor of Kiev University, Sikorsky. With regard to the possibility that Yushchinsky was the victim of religious fanaticism on the part of a fanatical sect of Judaism, testimony was solicited from a professor Glagolev of the Kiev Theological Academy, Department of Hebrew Language; Professor Troyitsky of the St. Petersburg Theological Academy, Department of Hebrew Language and Biblical Archeology; and Justin Pranaitis, Master in Theology.

Expressing the certainty that the crime was meticulously planned and executed with technical precision, Sikorsky ruled out the involvement of a mentally deranged person or persons. Sikorsky found in the murder procedure three distinct aims: to extract the largest quantity of blood, to cause excruciating pain, and finally to cause the victim's death. Such murders were recorded from time to time in Russia and other countries and were symptomatic of "racial vengeance" or a "vendetta by the sons of Jacob." The fact that children and youths were singled out for this type of murder seemed to suggest that they might be religiously motivated.

Professors Glagolev and Troyitsky rejected the possibility that, on the basis of Jewish belief as expressed in the Bible and the Talmud, Jews resort to the use of human blood, including Christian blood, for religiously motivated ritual purposes. According to Professor Glagolev, the prohibition against the spilling and the use of human blood in food, as laid down in the Laws of Moses, has never been modified or changed. If such unverified instances of the use of blood by Jews did occur, it was contrary to Judaic law.

Professor Troyitsky confirmed that the use of any kind of blood in food is forbidden by Judaic written law. Oral law allowed the use of blood from fish and locusts; also allowable is the use of blood for medicinal purposes upon a doctor's orders. The killing of a human being, Jew or non-Jew, is strictly forbidden, except in the event of war or as a punitive measure.

Pranaitis differed substantially from the opinions of Glagolev and Troyitsky. Basing his opinion on studying all sources of Jewish theology, he came to the conclusion that in Judaism there exists a so-called "dogma of blood." All rabbinic schools notwithstanding, their divergent views on various questions are at one in their hostility to non-Jews, who according to the Talmud were not considered human, but "animals in human image." The feeling of animosity nurtured by Jews, in keeping with their religious laws, to people of other nationalities or religion are especially pronounced in their attitude toward Christians. The commandment "Thou shalt not kill," according to rabbinic interpretation, relates only to Jews, not to people of another faith. Extermination of non-Jews is regarded as a feat which may precipitate the coming of the Messiah.

Pranaitis drew his conclusions primarily from a book by the monk Neophite, formerly a rabbi, who converted to Christianity. Neophite explained that Jews are in the habit of mixing Christian blood in their Passover dishes. The mode of putting a Christian to death is prescribed in the teachings of Kabbalah as follows: The victim's mouth should be sealed tight like an animal's who dies without a sound. There should be 13 stabs or incisions. Pranaitis concluded that Yushchinsky's murder and the timing of the crime strongly suggested a ritual slaying by Jews. The use and utilization of Christian blood represents a strict and dreadful secret, not known to all Jews, only to rabbis, bookish people, and the Pharisees. This secret is verbally communicated from a father to one of his sons, the latter being obliged to take a solemn oath not to reveal it to anyone—not even one's brothers.

The circumstances of the case leading to the conclusion of Beilis's involvement in the murder of Yushchinsky rest on the following information elicited in the preliminary hearings. As mentioned above, Yushchinsky left his home the last time in the early morning of March 12. Before leaving he took with him books and copybooks, yet he never appeared at school. Inasmuch as Yushchinsky had no gunpowder left for use in his toy gun and several days earlier had told his grandmother, Olympiada Nezhinsky, that he needed to obtain gunpowder from someone in Kiev, Mrs. Nezhinsky assumed that on March 12 prior to going to school he was looking for gunpowder. It subsequently turned out that instead of proceeding on that day to school, located in the center of town, Yushchinsky went to Lukyanovka.

In April, Zhenya Cheberyak told the student Vladimir Golubev that on the morning of March 12 Yushchinsky came to see him and they went for a walk in the Berner estate. In subsequent conversations with Golubev, Zhenya Cheberyak started denying that he had met that day with Yushchinsky. However, the initial information provided by young Cheberyak to Golubev was confirmed by testimony from Kazimir and Yuliana Shachovsky, who stated that on that particular day at nine in the morning they had seen Yushchinsky with Cheberyak. At first the boys were seen by Yuliana Shachovsky as they were standing on the corner of Upper Yurkovsky and Polovetsky Streets, eating candy, and sometime later they were observed near the Cheberyak home by Kazimir Shachovsky. At that time, Yushchinsky held in his hand a jar containing a black powder which Shachovsky assumed was gunpowder given him by Cheberyak.

The site on which Zhenya Cheberyak and his parents lived adjoins on one side the brick factory of Zaitsev, which is adjacent to the Berner estate, where Yushchinsky's body was discovered. On the Zaitsev estate lived the factory clerk, Menachem Mendel Teviev Beilis, and nearby was located a saddlery workshop, where awls were on hand. A fence surrounding the Zaitsev estate was in disrepair in some places, and it was possible to penetrate into the estate from where Cheberyak lived. Children had been wont to enter and play on the estate.

Kazimir Shachovsky testified that about three days after March

12, he met Zhenya Cheberyak on the street and asked him how was his walk with Yushchinsky on the day he had seen them together. Zhenya replied that they did not have a real good time, as when they were playing on the Zaitsev estate near the brick kiln, they were frightened away by a man with a black beard. Giving his testimony before the magistrate, Kazimir Shachovsky stated that in his opinion the man with the black beard was the clerk of the brick factory, Mendel. At the same time he offered the opinion that Mendel Beilis took part in the murder of Yushchinsky and that Zhenya Cheberyak lured Yushchinsky into the site of the brick factory.

Yuliana Shachovsky, wife of Kazimir, deposed that an acquaintance of hers, Anna, nicknamed "Volkivna," in talking about the Yushchinsky murder, told her, in the presence of a boy named Nicolai Kaluzny, that when Zhenya Cheberyak, Yushchinsky, and another unidentified boy played on the Zaitsev estate, a black-bearded man living there grabbed Yushchinsky before her very eyes and dragged him toward the brick kiln. Volkivna then named that man, saying that it was the clerk of the brick factory, Mendel.

Anna Volkivna, whose real family name is Zacharov, shrugged off Shachovsky's statement, denying that she had the above-mentioned conversation. The boy, Nicolai Kaluzny, also denied at first having heard the conversation with Mrs. Zacharov, but subsequently admitted that in his presence, Mrs. Zacharov, in chatting with Mrs. Shachovsky, said that she had seen a man with a black beard dragging the boy toward the kiln.

Yuliana Shachovsky, appearing inebriated, told an investigator in the case, Adam Polishchuk, that her husband, Kazimir, had personally seen on March 12th Mendel Beilis dragging Yushchinsky toward the kiln. Questioned about her statement to the investigator, Yuliana Shachovsky announced that she couldn't recall what she said, having been drunk, adding that her husband had never told her about seeing Beilis dragging Yushchinsky. Kazimir Shachovsky had also denied the incident. The Shachovskys had been questioned several times and kept changing their testimony.

Zhenya Cheberyak, in testimony before the magistrate, explained that the last time he had seen Yushchinsky was some ten days prior to the discovery of his body. He stated that Yushchinsky visited him about 2:00 P.M., inviting him to join him for a walk, but Zhenya declined and Yushchinsky left. Subsequently, Zhenya changed his testimony, saying that Yushchinsky came to him at that time, asking for gunpowder. Since Zhenya did not have any gunpowder to fulfill Yushchinsky's request, the latter left alone.

Summoned to the hearing as the defendant accused in concert with others of having participated in Yushchinsky's murder, Mendel Beilis did not admit his guilt, denying the crime attributed to him.

While in prison, Beilis shared a cell for a time with one Kozachenko, who was released from prison on November 11. Before Kozachenko was freed, the prison warden, Omelyanovsky, wishing to check whether Kozachenko was carrying any written messages from any of the prisoners, demanded from Kozachenko that he surrender such written messages in his possession. After some hesitation, Kozachenko handed him a letter written by Beilis to his wife.

"Dear Wife, please accept the bearer of this message," wrote Beilis, "as one of your own. He can help you a great deal in my behalf. I feel that I cannot hold out in jail much longer. If the man will ask you for money, give him whatever expenses that will be necessary. These are my enemies who lie about me in their testimonies." The letter was signed by Beilis with a postscript in his own hand: "You can fully rely on this person, just as I can."

The letter was forwarded to the magistrate on the day of Kozachenko's release from jail, and the investigator promptly interrogated Kozachenko about the circumstances of the letter entrusted to him. Kozachenko explained that he had several conversations with Beilis in prison about the Yushchinsky case. Seeking Kozachenko's help, Beilis proposed that he poison two of the witnesses and bribe a third one—for a monetary reward. The third witness Beilis did not identify by name, saying that he lived in the village called Obuhova, or hails from there. He also mentioned persons nicknamed "Frog" and "Lamplighter." What the "Frog" knew, Beilis did not say, but the "Lamplighter" ostensibly saw him walking with the late Yushchinsky. Before Kozachenko was released from prison, Beilis handed him the note to his wife, written by prisoner Puhalsky but dictated by Beilis, with the observation that upon receipt of this note, his wife would turn over to him the money collected by the "Jewish nation" concerned with the outcome of this case, which money is to be used for expenses in locating the witnesses who ought to be eliminated in the manner described above. From Jews, Beilis would obtain the poison (strychnine) to implement this proposal. Beilis did not specify the amount of the reward, but indicated that Kozachenko would get up to 500 rubles for expenses, and if he successfully fulfilled his assignment, he would receive "so much money as to last him a lifetime." Referring to the "Frog" and "Lamplighter," Beilis did not identify them by name.

From available testimony it was evident that the nickname "Frog" was linked to Mikhail Nakonechny and "Lamplighter" to Kazimir Shachovsky, who had been working for a contractor charged with lighting the kerosene lamps on several streets, including Upper Yurkovskaya Street. Nakonechny had been summoned to testify at several hearings and gave evidence favorable to Beilis. At one such hearing, he stated that Kazimir Shachovsky, on his way to an interrogation, said that he would "implicate" Mendel in the Yushchinsky case, since he had told the detectives that he, Shachovsky, stole wood from the Zaitsev factory.

As already reported, Shachovsky had, inter alia, recounted his conversation with Zhenya Cheberyak about a black-bearded man having scared Zhenya and Yushchinsky when they were playing on the Zaitsev estate. In the words of Zhenya's father, Vassily Cheberyak, Zhenya told him that several days before the discovery of Yushchinsky's body, he played with Andrey on the Zaitsev estate, when they were chased by Mendel Beilis but escaped. In addition, Vassily Cheberyak testified that about a week prior to that incident, when Yushchinsky's body was found, Zhenya, coming home from the Zaitsev estate, told him that Beilis was visited by two Jews in strange attire. Zhenya saw these Jews as they were praying. Immediately thereafter, when the news about Yushchinsky's murder was announced, the Jews left Beilis's apartment.

It was impossible to question Zhenya Cheberyak concerning the two visiting Jews, as this information reached the magistrate only after Zhenya's sudden demise from an attack of dysentery on August 8, 1911. However, Zhenya's sister, 9-year-old Ludmilla, confirmed the story about the aforementioned Jews at a subsequent hearing. According to her, she and Zhenya, going to fetch milk from Beilis, saw in his home two Jews who frightened them very much. She noticed one of them wearing a black cape and a black high hat on his head. In addition, Ludmilla told the magistrate that the last time she saw Yushchinsky was a week prior to the discovery of his body. Yushchinsky came to the house about eight o'clock in the morning and invited Zhenya to go to the Zaitsev estate in order to take a ride on the clay mixer. With Yushchinsky and Zhenya were also she, Ludmilla, her younger sister Valentina, and several other children, of whom she remembered Yevdokia Nakonechny. Slipping through a hole in the fence into the factory grounds, they started riding on the clay mixer, when suddenly they saw Mendel Beilis and two other Jews running toward them. The children jumped off the clay mixer and started running. Ludmilla and the other children closest to the fence managed to hide, but Yushchinsky and Zhenya were overtaken and grabbed by Beilis. Zhenya somehow twisted himself loose and escaped, but Yushchinsky, as she observed, was pulled by the hand by Beilis in the direction of the factory kiln. Her sister, Valya (Valentina), who could not run as fast as she and thus spent more time within the factory enclave, told her that she saw Yushchinsky being dragged toward the kiln by Beilis and two other Jews who were chasing the children.

Yevdokia Nakonechny, conceding that she had on several occasions taken rides on the clay mixer with other children, including Yushchinsky, and that they were frequently yelled at by the factory workers, deposed that she could not recall the incident of Beilis chasing them away. Valentina Cheberyak was not questioned. Becoming sick suddenly, almost simultaneously with her brother, Zhenya, she died of dysentery several days after her brother's demise.

Mendel Beilis's deposition indicated that he knew neither Yushchinsky nor Zhenya Cheberyak, although he did know the latter's mother. He worked as a clerk in the Zaitsev factory and on occasion he had to chase away from the factory grounds children engaged in all kinds of games. Jews in unusual attire did not visit him. His father was a *hasid*, but he himself was not religious and worked on the Sabbath. Some five years ago, he traveled from Kiev to the Zaitsev estate to observe the baking of matzos. They distributed the matzos to Zaitsev's relatives in Kiev, together with Passover wine. He did give a letter to Kozachenko to deliver to his wife, but he never asked him to poison or bribe any of the witnesses. Kozachenko assured Beilis that he might help him, telling him that he knew from the newspapers the testimonies of the "Frog" and the "Lamplighter." The letter to his wife was written for him by Alexander Puhalsky and in that letter Beilis wanted to ask his wife to give Kozachenko some money for delivering the letter and not for expenses in the search for witnesses.

On the basis of the aforementioned, Menachem Mendel Teviev Beilis, of the City of Vasilkova, Kiev Region, 39 years of age, was accused that in concert with other unidentified persons, with premeditated intent fed by religious fanaticism and ritual aims, he took the life of Andrey Yushchinsky, age 13, on March 12, 1911 in the City of Kiev within the grounds of the Zaitsev brick factory located on Upper Urkovsky Street, having seized Andrey Yushchinsky who was playing there with other children, carried him off into the factory premises, where with Beilis's accomplices and with his knowledge and consent tied Yushchinsky's hands, gagged him, and caused his death by inflicting seventeen wounds with a sharp instrument on his head, neck, body, such wounds being accompanied by heavy and prolonged suffering and causing almost total hemorrhaging. In consequence thereof and pursuant to Section 201 of the Criminal Code, Menachem Mendel Teviev Beilis was placed under the jurisdiction of the Kiev Circuit Court sitting with a jury.

PRESIDING JUDGE TO BEILIS: Do you admit your guilt in that (repeats the foregoing)?

BEILIS: No, not guilty. I earn an honest living. By work I sustain my wife and five children. Suddenly I was arrested. This never happened.

PRESIDING JUDGE: You will have the right in the course of the trial to offer clarifications. You have lawyers, but the law gives you the right to question the witnesses; also to make statements to the court, should you so desire. You can also petition the court to advise you about some aspect of the investigation. In such cases, direct your request to me and I will give you permission. Sit down please.

3

Maze of Contradictions

Mrs. Chachovsky was called to testify that she was acquainted with Mrs. Prihodko, the murdered boy's mother. While waiting in the court's anteroom, she witnessed how Vera Cheberyak, sitting in the same room, was trying to coach the boy, Zarutsky, to change his testimony to conform with Cheberyak's account about the incident at the Zaitsev estate where Beilis chased and seized Andrey Yushchinsky. The boy refused, saying, "Beilis didn't chase anyone." The prosecution intervened, dismissing Mrs. Chachovsky's story as "hearsay evidence."

Testimony of Mrs. Chachovsky
September 28, 1913

PRESIDING JUDGE: What do you know about this case?
WITNESS: I don't know anything. Still on the 25th I saw here Vera Cheberyak when she called over the boy Zarutsky and

started to coach him. Cheberyak said to him, "You tell in court that the three of us went to the brick factory, I, Zhenya Cheberyak, and Andrey Yushchinsky. We were chased. The two of us escaped but Andrey was seized.

QUESTION BY ZAMISLOVSKI: Did this occur here in court?

WITNESS: Yes.

PROSECUTOR: Were you questioned by the investigator?

WITNESS: No.

PROSECUTOR: This conversation with Cheberyak. How long ago was it?

WITNESS: It was here on the 25th.

PROSECUTOR: I didn't understand you. What you are saying is right here in the courtroom, you saw Cheberyak and talked to her?

WITNESS: Yes. She was sitting across from me. Then she summoned the boy Zarutsky and told him, "Here is what you tell them. That there were three of you. Zhenya, Andrey, and I. Tell them that you managed to tear yourself away from the chaser's hands."

PROSECUTOR: Whose hands?

WITNESS: Beilis's hands. "But Yushchinsky remained. Tell them that he grabbed him and dragged him." The boy answered, "I wouldn't tell that. I will tell that I sneaked into the factory site to steal some wood and some worker chased me away. Beilis didn't chase me."

PROSECUTOR: Who else heard this interchange?

WITNESS: There were many there.

PROSECUTOR: Name at least two of the others.

WITNESS: If I could see them face-to-face I would, but this way I can't.

PROSECUTOR: What were you invited to testify about?

WITNESS: I received a summons to testify that I knew Yushchinsky's mother and nothing else.

PROSECUTOR: You were thus invited on account of his mother? I ask the court to put it in the record the news she advised us about.

Deacon Dimitry Mochugovsky tutored Yushchinsky at the request of his mother for 10 rubles per month. The deacon took charge of the funeral of Yushchinsky. He testified that he noticed leaflets being distributed at the funeral, accusing Jews of the murder and calling for a pogrom. Zarudny, one of Beilis's lawyers, asked the court to produce one of the leaflets as being relevant to the case.

PROSECUTOR: We are dealing with the murder of Yushchinsky and not with leaflets being distributed at the cemetery. The demand that the leaflets be produced is without merit.

The court decided to deny the request of the defense to produce a copy of the leaflets.

At age 19, Vladimir Golubev, a slim, handsome, but high-strung student of Kiev University was already an influential leader of the Double-Headed Eagle organization and of the Union of the Russian People.

In his trial testimony, Golubev acknowledged that he had gained his information about Jews from reading the writings of one Lutostansky, a discredited anti-Semitic pamphleteer and a defrocked priest, which knowledge reinforced his belief that Jews habitually used Christian blood in their religious practices. Golubev was a protégé of the rightist member of the Duma, Zamislovski, a close associate of Minister of Justice Shcheglovitov, which "connection" endowed him with the political clout to intrude into the Yushchinsky murder investigation and steer it in the direction of the Jews. Impatient with the slow pace of the investigation, Golubev petitioned the governor of Kiev to expel three thousand Jews from that city—the names of the Jews to be furnished by the Double-Headed Eagle organization. The governor demurred but sought guidance from the minister of justice. Shcheglovitov praised the young student for his "loyalty and patriotism" in the pursuit of "common objectives," but advised him "not to rush things."

Brandorf, state attorney for the Kiev superior court, and one of the few officials of the justice department, who was not corrupted or intimidated by his employer, Shcheglovitov, testified that "parallel

with the official investigation was a private one, carried on by
Golubev with the knowledge of Chaplinsky (state prosecutor, Kiev
appellate court) . . . He (Golubev) was the inventor of the Beilis
case . . . I pointed out to Chaplinsky on many occasions that this was
an impossible situation, that according to my information, Golubev
was using illegal methods and intentionally hindering police activities . . ." Chaplinsky warned Brandorf that tampering with Golubev
and his crowd was a "highly risky business."

In his testimony at the trial, Golubev, a major witness for the
prosecution, disclosed the fact that at his first encounter with
Zhenya Cheberyak the latter admitted having been with Andrey
Yushchinsky on March 12, the day of the murder. When Golubev
sought further corroboration, Cheberyak's son ran away when he
tried to approach him. When Cheberyak was arrested, Golubev
stormed into police headquarters, demanding her release, arguing
that Vera Cheberyak "belonged" to the Union of the Russian People.

Testimony of Vladimir Golubev
September 30, 1913

WITNESS: I went to Yushchinsky's funeral because I wanted to
see his mother, who was somehow suspected in the case. I was
anxious to clarify the attitude of the relatives toward the boy.
I started making inquiries among the boys in the neighborhood
and incidentally met Zhenya Cheberyak. He told me that he
knew Andrey very well, that he was his friend, and that he saw
him on the twelfth of March. Andrey came to him in the
morning and they went for a walk. At that time I had no idea
that I would have to testify about it, since I gathered information for myself. When I tried to question him a second time,
Zhenya kept running away, yet I did get to talk to him, at

which time he said he knew nothing about Yushchinsky, except that he did visit him, but a long time ago. I assumed that someone told him to keep his mouth shut. Then I went over to see Natalia Yushchinsky, the murdered boy's mother. My intention was to go with her to the cave and learn from her the circumstances surrounding the discovery of the body and the condition of the body. The boy was found to be in a half-sitting position, wearing a shirt, underpants, but no socks. Next to him there was a jacket soiled in clay, the clay having been of two sorts—grey and yellow. The clay in the cave was yellow. The grey clay corresponds to that found in the Zaitsev factory.

PROSECUTOR: You've seen it yourself?

WITNESS: No, I did not. Yushchinsky's mother received a letter addressed either from Kharkov or Cherson. The letter, signed "Christian," indicated that near the Lukyanovsky Church of St. Theodore, an unknown man had seen a boy of the religious school, and nearby stood an old and young Jew. The old man holding his hand and the young one was talking. This letter was turned over to the commander of the criminal division, but the commander dismissed it as outright "foolishness." I informed the magistrate about the letter in May, but in early May the magistrate still did not have the letter. Subsequently I met a boy whose name I did not know who said that he too saw a Jew with a boy. Becoming more familiar with the case, it occurred to me that the murder resembled those perpetrated by Jews for ritual purposes. In addition I became increasingly convinced that what is described in the book by Lutostansky conforms with the evidence found on the body. I was then fully persuaded that we are dealing with a ritual murder perpetrated for known aims. I then started inquiring whether Yushchinsky had any contacts with "kikes." It turned out that at the factory there lived a certain Mendel. I proceeded questioning people about Mendel and was told that he lived at the factory a long time and had been always chasing children away from the factory. It was noticed, however, that following the murder his attitude mellowed so that he started giving the children candy. I reported that to the commander of the criminal division and he again said, "Foolishness." Afterwards, in talking to Krasovsky, the latter said that the murder was committed by Jews in collaboration with relatives. I was eager to get more information on Beilis. I learned that Beilis traveled annually to another Zaitsev estate for matzos. It then dawned on me that the investigation was drawing to a close and that a trial was about to begin and that Beilis would be defended by the best lawyers. We held a consultation leading to a decision to invite, as private prosecutors to represent Yushchinsky's mother, Shmakov and Zamislovski. Mrs. Yushchinsky agreed. I went to Petersburg and secured the services of Shmakov and Zamislovski.

SHMAKOV: How was Beilis treated at the factory?

WITNESS: He was treated respectfully because he was a *tzadik*. (Beilis burst out laughing.)

SHMAKOV: Did you talk to anyone about such a sect?

WITNESS: I was absolutely convinced that "*hasids*" and *tzadiks* used Christian blood. I started reading various books, some of which I borrowed from Father Serapion. I read the works of Lutostansky.

KARABCHESKY TO PRESIDING JUDGE: I request that Golubev's testimony be placed in the record. Specifically his conviction that this was indisputably a ritual murder, this conviction being based upon the wounds inflicted on the late boy and the information elicited from books by Lutostansky on the subject.

SHMAKOV: I would like to add in the record that not only Lutostansky's book deals with the subject but also the essays of Neophite.

In their depositions before the magistrate, the "Lamplighters," Kazimir and Yuliana Shachovsky, who serviced the petroleum lamps on several neighborhood streets, claimed that a certain "Volkivna" (wolf woman), a derelict and alcoholic, had told them that she had seen a "bearded man," presumably Beilis, seizing Andrey Yushchinsky on the premises of the Zaitsev estate and dragging him toward the brick factory kiln.

In their testimony at the trial, they repudiated their allegations about "Beilis dragging Andrey," admitting that they had been plied with vodka by detectives Polishchuk and Vygranov, who had coached them to implicate Beilis. Their trial testimony revealed that they had seen Andrey Yushchinsky and Zhenya Cheberyak together on March 12, the day of the murder. Andrey was wearing a jacket, a regulation cap, and an overcoat, but carried no books. That Zhenya Cheberyak had seen Andrey on the day of the murder—a fact Zhenya and his mother, Vera Cheberyak, had emphatically denied—reinforced the contention of the defense that the murder was committed at Cheberyak's flat, and not on the Zaitzev estate.

Testimony of Kazimir Shachovsky

PRESIDING JUDGE: Tell the court all you know about this case.

SHACHOVSKY: On Saturday, March 12th, sometime between nine and ten o'clock in the morning, while crossing Upper Yurkovskaya Street, I saw Zhenya Cheberyak with Andrey Yushchinsky.

PROSECUTOR: Are you a lamplighter?

SHACHOVSKY: Yes, sir.

PROSECUTOR: Do you recall precisely that it was on the twelfth of March that you saw Yushchinsky with Zhenya Cheberyak? Did you know Andrey from before?

SHACHOVSKY: I knew him.

PROSECUTOR: What made you remember that particular day? Were you on the way to get petrol?

SHACHOVSKY: Yes, sir.

PROSECUTOR: Where did you go for the petrol?

SHACHOVSKY: To Balashov.

PROSECUTOR: Did you on that occasion get some advance on your salary?

SHACHOVSKY: I received a ruble.

PROSECUTOR: What time was it when you went for the petrol?

SHACHOVSKY: Around seven in the morning.

PROSECUTOR: You can verify the fact that on that day you received a ruble?

SHACHOVSKY: Yes, sir, I can.

PROSECUTOR: Was it the factory siren that told you the precise time you crossed Yurkovskaya Street? Did you hear the siren?

SHACHOVSKY: Yes, I heard it.

PROSECUTOR: How many siren whistles are there? Three?

SHACHOVSKY: Yes, one at six o'clock, one at six-thirty and the last one at seven o'clock.

PROSECUTOR: So you heard the seven o'clock siren?

SHACHOVSKY: Yes.

PROSECUTOR: Do you live next door to Vera Cheberyak?

SHACHOVSKY: Yes, I live at number thirty-eight on Yurkovskaya and she lives at number forty.

PROSECUTOR: Was the liquor store open at that time?

SHACHOVSKY: Yes, it was open.

PROSECUTOR: When does it open?

SHACHOVSKY: At eight.

PROSECUTOR: Is that where Mrs. Malitsky works?

SHACHOVSKY: Yes, sir.

PROSECUTOR: What did Andrey wear on his head?

SHACHOVSKY: A uniform cap.

PROSECUTOR: Did you tell an investigator that you'd seen Andrey on March twelfth?

SHACHOVSKY: Yes, I told it to Krasovsky.

PROSECUTOR: Did you see Zhenya afterwards?

SHACHOVSKY: Some three to four days thereafter.

PROSECUTOR: Did you ask him about his walk with Andrey—where they were headed?

SHACHOVSKY: Yes, he said they walked over to the Zaitsev estate.

PROSECUTOR: What else did he tell you?

SHACHOVSKY: He said they were chased away from there.

PROSECUTOR: Who chased them?

SHACHOVSKY: Some unknown person.

PROSECUTOR: Did he describe the person chasing him? Did he have a beard?

SHACHOVSKY: No. Definitely no beard.

PROSECUTOR: Didn't you tell the investigator that you didn't come forward before because you were afraid to get involved?

SHACHOVSKY: (Silent)

PROSECUTOR: Did you know Beilis?

SHACHOVSKY: I knew that he worked at the brick factory.

PROSECUTOR: Did you see him at any time, talk to him?

SHACHOVSKY: I saw him on the street, but never talked to him.

PROSECUTOR: Didn't he suspect you of stealing wood from the estate?

SHACHOVSKY: I don't know, people were talking . . .

SHMAKOV: Didn't you tell the investigator that there was a third boy with Zhenya and Andrey? Was Beilis's son with them?

SHACHOVSKY: I didn't even mention Beilis's son.

SHMAKOV: Didn't you tell the investigator that Beilis and Cheberyak were on good terms?

SHACHOVSKY: I can't say they were on good terms.

SHMAKOV: Didn't you tell the investigator that Zhenya referred to a man with a black beard who had chased them away?

SHACHOVSKY: I can't say.

SHMAKOV: Are you denying it?

SHACHOVSKY: I can't deny it, maybe I did say that. I was pestered, the detectives gave me no peace, every day I received a new summons.

SHMAKOV: You indicated that you were beaten—who beat you?

SHACHOVSKY: I don't know, they called me dirty names . . .

SHMAKOV: Didn't you ask the investigator why he doesn't question Zhenya Cheberyak, who knows much more about it?

SHACHOVSKY: (Silent)

ZAMISLOVSKI: Didn't you change your story every time?

SHACHOVSKY: (Silent)

KARABCHEVSKY: You were questioned by detectives?

SHACHOVSKY: (Silent)

KARABCHEVSKY: What did they advise you to say? Didn't they tell you to implicate Beilis?

SHACHOVSKY: They plied me with vodka, told me to say this and that . . .

KARABCHEVSKY: Didn't they tell you to testify against Beilis?

SHACHOVSKY: Yes, they did.

KARABCHEVSKY: You said you were beaten up. Were these Russians who beat you, or were they Jews?

SHACHOVSKY: Russians.

SHMAKOV: Did you testify that on orders from his mother, Zhenya Cheberyak would not tell the truth?

SHACHOVSKY: Yes, I did.

Katerina Dyakonov testified that she visited Vera Cheberyak on March 11 and March 12, the day Andrey Yushchinsky was murdered. On March 11, she saw Andrey coming in looking for Zhenya Cheberyak, his friend. Zhenya ushered him into the small room in front. When Katerina left the Cheberyak flat at 3:00 in the afternoon, Andrey was still there.

On March 12, when Katerina entered the Cheberyak home, she witnessed three persons scampering out from one room into another, whom she identified as Rudzinsky, Latyshev, and Singayevsky, the three criminals whom the defense had accused as the perpetrators of the murder of Yushchinsky.

An important piece of evidence was the bloodstained pillowcase found on Yushchinsky's body. Katerina Dyakonov identified the pillowcase as the one she had embroidered for Vera Cheberyak.

Testimony of Katerina Dyakonov

PRESIDING JUDGE: Please tell us what you know about this case. You've taken an oath to tell only the truth?

DYAKONOV: I became acquainted with Vera Cheberyak in 1909, but it was a year later that we started visiting each other's home. She once invited me to her home, saying that she wanted me to meet her new friends, identifying them as "good people"—doctors, professors, etc. I agreed. We played "post office" and exchanged notes. I received one note that I found offensive and wanted to know who sent it. Having received no reply, I left.

PRESIDING JUDGE: Did you visit her after this incident?

DYAKONOV: Yes, I did.

PRESIDING JUDGE: Tell us your experiences when you spent the night there.

DYAKONOV: That was on March thirteenth.

PRESIDING JUDGE: Did you sleep in your clothes?

DYAKONOV: I don't recall if I undressed or not.

PRESIDING JUDGE: Tell us what happened on the eleventh of March?

DYAKONOV: It was approximately twelve noon when I got there. We drank tea. Around two o'clock there was a knock on the door and Vera went to open the door. I asked who was it, and she said "the goblin," Zhenya's friend. Vera went to fetch Zhenya, who invited his friend in and led him into the small room in front.

PRESIDING JUDGE: This was all on the eleventh of March?

DYAKONOV: Yes.

PRESIDING JUDGE: Weren't the children planning to visit Grandma on March twelfth?

DYAKONOV: No, they were all planning to look for switches. I asked Zhenya to cut me one and he said he would. The following day, I visited Cheberyak again. Vera opened the door and I saw three men—seemingly surprised—scampering into the small room and slamming the door shut. Vera wouldn't let me into the dining room, ushering me into the kitchen. After a while, I left for home.

PROSECUTOR: What's your profession?

DYAKONOV: I sew. I am a dressmaker.

PROSECUTOR: You have a sister Ksenia?

DYAKONOV: Yes.

PROSECUTOR: Did you see many people at the Cheberyak home, when you visited her?

DYAKONOV: No, only that one time.

PROSECUTOR: How many persons were there?

DYAKONOV: I'd say about eleven.

PROSECUTOR: So that was the first time you've seen Yushchinsky?

DYAKONOV: Yes, the first time.

PROSECUTOR: On that day, when Yushchinsky, or "the goblin," walked in, how long did you stay there?

DYAKONOV: Until about three o'clock.

PROSECUTOR: And when you left, Yushchinsky was still there?

DYAKONOV: Yes.

PROSECUTOR: Who were the three persons who rushed out from one room into another? Did you know them?

DYAKONOV: Singayevsky, Rudzinsky, and Latyshev.

PROSECUTOR: Did you notice at that time, was the carpet suspiciously rolled up?

DYAKONOV: The room was in disarray, the carpet thrown under the table.

PROSECUTOR: When you left, were the three men still there?

DYAKONOV: Yes.

PROSECUTOR: Were the children there, or did they visit their grandmother?

DYAKONOV: They were not there.

PROSECUTOR: All this transpired on the twelfth, and the following day Vera told you she had to go to the railroad station to dispatch a valise somewhere. On the fourteenth, she invited you again to spend the night at her place?

DYAKONOV: Yes.

PROSECUTOR: She only had one bed. Did you share the bed with her?

DYAKONOV: Yes.

PROSECUTOR: And that night, stretching your feet, you felt a hard object pressing on your toes?

DYAKONOV: I got frightened and woke up, but Vera said, "Go back to sleep, there's nothing to be afraid of."

PROSECUTOR: Weren't you interested to find out what that "hard object" was?

DYAKONOV: I didn't look around, but I noticed some articles piled up in the corner.

PROSECUTOR: This was on the fourteenth of March. On March twentieth Yushchinsky's corpse was found in the cave. Did you go to the cave?

DYAKONOV: No, Vera went.

PROSECUTOR: When you got frightened touching that unidentified object, did you tell that to the investigators?

DYAKONOV: No one asked me.

PROSECUTOR: When were you first questioned by Colonel Ivanove?

DYAKONOV: I don't remember.

PROSECUTOR: It was erased from your memory . . . and when did you first meet Krasovsky?

DYAKONOV: At the end of April, 1912.

PROSECUTOR: Did he inquire about your association with Cheberyak?

DYAKONOV: I told him all about it.

PROSECUTOR: You've met him several times with your sister. Where did you meet? At restaurants; did he take you to the theatre?

DYAKONOV: Yes.

PROSECUTOR: How long did these meetings take place?

DYAKONOV: Until May.

PROSECUTOR: Did you discuss the Yushchinsky case?

DYAKONOV: Yes.

PROSECUTOR: Didn't you tell Colonel Ivanove that you met four persons at the Cheberyak home, naming Lysunov as the fourth man?

DYAKONOV: I was mistaken. I saw only three.

PROSECUTOR: You also told Colonel Ivanove about your encounter with a masked man who told you the murder took place at the Cheberyak home. Didn't you question this phantom, where he got the information?

DYAKONOV: He would not tell me.

PROSECUTOR: Didn't you tell Krasovsky your own supposition that Yushchinsky's body was kept in Cheberyak's basement and that it was carried out by Mandzelevsky, Michalchuk, and Rudzinsky?

DYAKONOV: Yes.

PROSECUTOR: Didn't you know that they were in custody at that time?

DYAKONOV: No, I did not.

ZAMISLOVSKI: When you first met Andrey at the Cheberyaks, did he have books with him?

DYAKONOV: I don't recall the books, but he wore a coat.

ZAMISLOVSKI: On the twelfth of March, were you alone at the Cheberyaks, or was your sister with you?

DYAKONOV: I was alone.

ZAMISLOVSKI: Didn't you tell Krasovsky that Vera and Vassily Cheberyak practically admitted to you that the murder was "their job"?

DYAKONOV: Yes, they told me. Vassily Cheberyak said that

there was a book out about the Yushchinsky murder, and I said, "I have no money for books," then I said, "Didn't some kike do it?" And Vassily Cheberyak said, "You really don't get it, do you, that our 'boys' did it."

ZAMISLOVSKI: Those were his exact words—that our boys did it; yet prior to this conversation, you thought that some kike did it?

DYAKONOV: I said that to find out what he had thought.

ZAMISLOVSKI: Didn't you have a premonition that the boy's body was hidden at the Cheberyak flat?

DYAKONOV: I did have that suspicion.

ZAMISLOVSKI: But you did say that some kike did it.

DYAKONOV: I only said that to get his opinion. I didn't believe it.

ZAMISLOVSKI: What else did he say?

DYAKONOV: He said it was done to provoke a pogrom.

ZAMISLOVSKI: Didn't you also talk to Luda (Ludmilla)?

DYAKONOV: Yes, Luda said that when Yushchinsky was being killed, mother was on the staircase. I said, "What did they kill him with," and she said, "With awls."

ZAMISLOVSKI: How long did you know Colonel Ivanove?

DYAKONOV: A long time, since 1911.

ZAMISLOVSKI: Were you his agent?

DYAKONOV: No, I only reported to him what I knew.

ZAMISLOVSKI: Did you get paid?

DYAKONOV: Occasionally he gave me money.

ZAMISLOVSKI: How much?

DYAKONOV: He used to give me five rubles.

ZAMISLOVSKI: You tell me that Ludmilla practically confessed to you how the crime was committed, that Vera was a "lookout" on the staircase, and that the murder weapon—the awls—were then thrown out to avoid suspicion?

DYAKONOV: Yes, Ludmilla asked me not to tell her mother, as Vera often beat her.

ZAMISLOVSKI: Did you report this to Colonel Ivanove?

DYAKONOV: I don't know if I did or not.

KARABCHEVSKY: When Valya got sick, did you have any talk with Vera about taking her to the hospital?

DYAKONOV: I told her that the child was gravely ill and required hospitalization, and she said that it was useless. She hardly took care of her.

ZAMISLOVSKI TO PRESIDING JUDGE: Your honor, I suggest that the witness be shown the pillowcase found on Yushchinsky's body. (Pillowcase is shown to the witness.)

DYAKONOV: Yes, that is Cheberyak's pillowcase.

ZAMISLOVSKI: You are confirming under oath that this is Cheberyak's pillowcase?

DYAKONOV: Yes, this is hers.

PRESIDING JUDGE: I wish to remind the jury that at the hearing before the magistrate this witness testified that the pillowcase was embroidered with red threads; now she is saying it was black.

What Ekaterina Dyakonov had seen at the Cheberyak home on the day of the murder, Zinaida Malitsky had heard. Residing in a flat directly below Cheberyak's for many years, Mrs. Malitsky had learned to distinguish the various sounds coming from the flat above. On the day of the murder, she had heard unusual noises emanating from Cheberyak's flat, sounds of steps of grown-up persons dragging a heavy object, which was preceded by a child's screams.

Testimony of Zinaida Malitsky

PRESIDING JUDGE: Tell us, please, what do you know about this case?

MALITSKY: About the Beilis case, I know nothing.

PRESIDING JUDGE: What do you know about the Yushchinsky murder?

MALITSKY: I know what I heard—that's a fact. I heard a suspicious noise, something out of the ordinary, a child's steps... whether she was murdering Yushchinsky or someone else, I don't know.

PRESIDING JUDGE: Give us details.

MALITSKY: This was at the beginning of March 1911, my husband was away. I heard at the Cheberyak flat above steps of a child, running from one room to another, then I heard a door being slammed, then a child's scream, more like a wail, then I heard the steps of adults moving toward the room where the cries came from, then I heard a whispered conversation, then a muffled cry. At that point, I had to rush out to the wine store where I worked, sold some wine, and returned to my home. I again heard the sound of heavy steps of adults, as if they were dancing—back and forth. I knew they were not Zhenya's steps because the boy wore boots and his steps sounded like those of an adult; nor were these the voices of the girls, with which I was familiar. I subsequently learned from a woman that she had met the Cheberyak children on the street.

PROSECUTOR: What's your occupation?

MALITSKY: I take care of a government wine store nearby.

PROSECUTOR: How many times were you questioned by the investigator?

MALITSKY: Fenenko questioned me once, Mashkevitz twice or more.

PROSECUTOR: When were you questioned the first time?

MALITSKY: I think it was in July.

PROSECUTOR: What did you tell the investigator then?

MALITSKY: I told him nothing.

PROSECUTOR: What about the second time?

MALITSKY: The second time I told him everything I knew.

PROSECUTOR: So the second time you recalled the episode you told us about?

MALITSKY: Yes, I did.

PROSECUTOR: You said that you could distinguish which steps were Zhenya's, which were Valya's, and which were Ludmilla's?

MALITSKY: Yes, I could.

PROSECUTOR: And you could identify the people by the sound of their voice?

MALITSKY: Yes, I could.

ZAMISLOVSKI: What time was it?

MALITSKY: I can't say for sure, around ten, eleven in the morning.

ZAMISLOVSKI: Can you be more specific as to what you've heard?

MALITSKY: I can't describe it in greater detail. I heard a commotion. I heard them dragging a heavy object from one room to another, I heard Vera's rasping voice . . . there were no more child's voices.

ZAMISLOVSKI: How many people would you say carried that heavy object?

MALITSKY: I'd say five or six, with Cheberyak in the middle.

ZAMISLOVSKI: So, Cheberyak also helped?

MALITSKY: Yes.

ZAMISLOVSKI: Did you hear perhaps the steps of the Dyakonov sisters walking?

MALITSKY: No, as I said, I kept running in and out of the store, someone might have come in.

ZAMISLOVSKI: What else did you hear after the commotion?

MALITSKY: I heard laughter and just banter.

GRUZENBERG: When your husband arrived home, did you tell him about this incident?

MALITSKY: Yes, he told me it was my duty as an honest citizen to report it to the authorities regardless of the repercussions.

GRUZENBERG: Did you know that Cheberyak traded in articles of gold and silver?

MALITSKY: She once offered to sell me a fur coat. I also saw her holding some jewelry. She offered me many things for sale.

GRUZENBERG: Didn't you ask her how a person of modest means could afford these things?

MALITSKY: She told me that the fur coat belonged to some person who was hospitalized.

KARABCHEVSKY: Are you still employed as a caretaker at the wine store?

MALITSKY: No, they let me go, presumably because they could not find me home, but it's clear to me that that was not the real reason.

KARABCHEVSKY: How long did you work at the store?

MALITSKY: Nine years.

ZARUDNY: You said that your husband advised you that as an honest citizen you ought to tell everything to the authorities regardless of the unpleasant consequences. How would telling the truth result in "unpleasant consequences"?

MALITSKY: Cheberyak threatened me, told me she'll scratch my eyes out—all because I had the temerity to ask her what happened.

PROSECUTOR: Were you on friendly terms with her?

MALITSKY: I was neither friendly nor unfriendly, but she used to find pretexts to attack me.

The testimony of A. D. Margolin, a prominent Jewish communal leader in Kiev and Beilis's initial attorney, is revealing in that it describes Vera Cheberyak's "mysterious" pilgrimage to Kharkov. One of her traveling companions, the journalist Brazul-Brushkovsky, maintained that Cheberyak had insisted on making the trip to consult with one of her criminal "friends," Lysunov, who—according to Cheberyak—was in prison in Kharkov, and who was in possession of important information relative to the Yush-chinsky murder. Brazul-Brushkovsky (also referred to as Brazul) had another purpose in mind. He was eager to have Cheberyak meet his friend Margolin, who as a criminal lawyer was more qualified to probe Vera's mind and assess her credibility. Margolin was reluctant to meet Cheberyak in his hometown, Kiev, lest such a meeting might "compromise" him. (And indeed the Kharkov trip resulted in his being summoned as a witness and thus barred from representing Beilis.) To Vera Cheberyak, Brazul represented Margolin as a member of the Duma who was in a position to help her in many ways. In her testimony before the magistrate and at the trial, Cheberyak alleged that at the Kharkov meeting, Margolin asked her to assume responsibility for the Yushchinsky murder and be compensated to the tune of 40,000 rubles and, if need be, provided with the best legal talent for her defense. Margolin and Brazul repeatedly and emphatically denied Cheberyak's allegations.

Testimony of A. D. Margolin
October 7, 1913

PRESIDING JUDGE: What do yo know about this case? How did your meeting with Cheberyak come about?

MARGOLIN: I became interested in this case only since November 1911. It's worth mentioning that until the fall the case attracted little attention in both Jewish and Christian circles. This is attributable, I believe, to the fact that relatives had been the early suspects. Only one small-circulation newspaper advanced the ritual-murder theme, and since the paper was promptly confiscated by the censor, the public was under the impression that the religious motive was discounted by the judicial authorities. The prevailing opinion was that this was an ordinary criminal case. I first became familiar with this case when I paid a visit to my friends on the staff of the newspaper *Kievskaya Mysel*. Among those, I was particularly close to Brazul-Brushkovsky, who impressed me with his honesty and integrity. Nevertheless, I initially treated the information he seemed to have had about this case with considerable skepticism, since Brazul has had no experience as a professional investigator and had, at times, displayed a quixotic streak—in the best sense of that term—in some of his journalistic ventures. I recall having been approached by Brazul some time in November to meet Vera Cheberyak. There was some talk at that time that this woman knew everything, and according to Brazul, Cheberyak's behavior had undergone a drastic change with the discovery of Yushchinsky's body.

PRESIDING JUDGE: When did that alleged change occur?

MARGOLIN: At the end of November. Cheberyak had complained to Brazul that while the investigators had initially treated her with respect, they subsequently viewed her as a "prime suspect." Brazul insisted that in view of my familiarity with criminal cases, it may prove advantageous if I talked to her. I declined on the ground that there was still no palpable interest in the case, and also because I had serious reservations about meeting a woman of such a shady reputation. I told Brazul that once he had acquired substantive information, which needed verification, I may then reconsider my refusal to see her. On one occasion, when I was on my way to consult with judicial authorities, I ran into a woman whose head was heavily bandaged and was told by one of the people on hand that the woman was Vera Cheberyak. The same evening, Brazul informed me that Vera Cheberyak had been severely beaten by one Miffle, and that she was eager to "expose" the Yushchinsky murder by naming Miffle as the perpetrator of the crime. According to Brazul, Cheberyak was ready to "spill the beans," but needed additional data which she could obtain only in the city of Kharkov. I then told Brazul that I was planning to go to Kharkov on business, and if he could arrange to bring Cheberyak to Kharkov at that time, I'd be prepared to see her incognito in my hotel room. Thus on December sixth I left for Kharkov, and after concluding my business at the

Kharkov district court, I returned to my hotel room. In the evening, I received a phone call from Brazul, informing me that he was in Kharkov with Cheberyak and that they were ready to come to see me. He indicated that a third person, Vygranov, would join them, assuring me that the latter was a trustworthy person and that Cheberyak insisted that he be present at the interview. I must say that for one who is zealous about his reputation, the presence of a third person posed a certain hazard. However, I reluctantly agreed to the arrangement. The trio appeared at my hotel room, and Cheberyak immediately monopolized the conversation. She said she traveled to Kharkov with only one purpose in mind—to retaliate against Miffle, who assaulted her, who poisoned her children, and who is determined to make her life miserable. She then disclosed that the murder took place in a cave a short distance from where the body was found, and that those participating in the homicide were Prihodko, Nezhinsky, Miffle, and Nazarenko. As to the motive, she stated that the boy had known of the criminal activities within the family and thus had to be silenced. I asked her only two questions: If the crime was committed as she had described it, why were there so many wounds on the boy's body, to which she replied, "Prihodko knows medicine." My second question was, "How do you know that it was Miffle who assaulted you, since it took place in total darkness and you did not identify the voice of your assailant?" Without hesitation, Cheberyak said that on the following day, her neighbors reported seeing two men, holding hands, fleeing from the spot where the assault took place. This is proof that one of the assailants was blind, she averred; hence it could have been only Miffle. This was the gist of the whole conversation. I believe that Brazul then said to Cheberyak, "Since you had indicated that you had to obtain information from someone in Kharkov, perhaps you ought to do it now, so you can let us have 'the whole picture,' " to which

I said, that in that case, "I'll make myself available to see you the following morning."

The next morning, the same trio paid me a second visit, but the meeting lasted only a few minutes, as Cheberyak had nothing new to report. I told Brazul there and then that I considered further meetings with Cheberyak superfluous. They left, and I departed for Kiev that evening. Several days thereafter, Brazul reported to me briefly the information elicited from Mrs. Malitsky. At that point, I was in possession of the following facts: Cheberyak's oft-repeated story centered exclusively on the complicity of the relatives—first the mother, then the stepfather and the uncle, and finally Miffle. When Beilis was arrested, Cheberyak's yarn about the relatives had come to an abrupt end. At that juncture, in reviewing the sequence of events, starting with the ill-fated trip to Kharkov, Cheberyak's ever-changing behavior, and the endless fluctuations in her story about the "relatives," who had been detained on suspicion and then released, and finally her fixation on Miffle, led me to the conclusion that Cheberyak was not only a witness, but a participant in the crime in one form or another. I shared this conclusion with Brazul, but he disagreed. Yet even in Kharkov, I gained the impression that Brazul had fallen under Cheberyak's spell and believed her implicitly. My advice to him was that inasmuch as he had been impressed with Cheberyak's credibility, he ought to share his beliefs with the court investigator, which, I understand, he did. In January, I was invited to be a defender in this case.

PROSECUTOR: What's your occupation?

MARGOLIN: I am an attorney.

PROSECUTOR: You testified that you had taken an interest in this case in November 1911 and not when Beilis was implicated.

MARGOLIN: When Beilis was arrested, it had been bruited about that it was the result of a misunderstanding related to his residence permit. It was only some time later that the Beilis arrest was linked to the Yushchinsky case.

PROSECUTOR: How long do you know Brazul?

MARGOLIN: I have known him for many years.

PROSECUTOR: When you both became involved in this case, was there any talk about your undertaking the Beilis defense? Who invited you to serve as his attorney?

MARGOLIN: At first, Beilis's wife and brother, and subsequently Beilis himself.

PROSECUTOR: Are you a homeowner?

MARGOLIN: No.

PROSECUTOR: Are you involved in Jewish communal affairs?

MAROGLIN: Yes, I am actively involved in Jewish affairs.

PROSECUTOR: Why were you, as a Jew, drawn to this case? Was it because the defendant was a Jew?

MARGOLIN: Yes.

PROSECUTOR: Was it through Brazul that you became acquainted with Krasovsky?

MARGOLIN: Very superficially.

PROSECUTOR: But you did know him?

MARGOLIN: Who didn't?

PROSECUTOR: I, for instance, did not.

MARGOLIN: That's because you are not a Kiev resident. As to my connection with Beilis, I would like to add that there was a general impression in the city that Beilis would not be brought to trial.

PROSECUTOR: But when Beilis was brought to trial, your beliefs were shaken, weren't they? So on December 6th, you traveled to Kharkov still not being the accredited Beilis attorney?

MARGOLIN: I had every reason to believe that I would be invited to serve in that capacity.

PROSECUTOR: That was your supposition?

MARGOLIN: Yes, indeed, inasmuch as I was called upon to participate in every Jewish case in this region.

PROSECUTOR: You testified that in the course of your encounter with Cheberyak, you managed to interject only two questions?

MARGOLIN: I found no need to pose any other questions.

PROSECUTOR: What did she tell you, that you found of particular interest?

MARGOLIN: I was frankly amazed that her story was so devoid of substance. Had she indicated that she wanted to clear up the circumstances of the murder on condition that she be properly rewarded, I might have believed her.

PROSECUTOR: So she pointed to Miffle as the one who beat her up, and in order to avenge her honor, she decided to go to Kharkov?

MARGOLIN: That's not entirely correct. She said she went to Kharkov in order to consult with some criminals.

PROSECUTOR: Where did Brazul get the money to cover the travel expenses for three people?

MARGOLIN: I have a notion that he may have received some advance remuneration from national newspapers for exclusive coverage of the trial; but that's strictly speculation on my part.

PROSECUTOR: I am puzzled about Cheberyak's motives for the Kharkov trip.

MARGOLIN: I have formed a definite opinion about her trip, which, I believe, can be construed as evidence about her complicity in the crime.

PROSECUTOR: So you regard it as evidence. Perhaps she was just interested to meet a person of means. Aren't you a person of means?

MARGOLIN: If absolutely necessary, I can report that I am sustained by my own labors, but my family does have other sources of income. Surely, you can easily make inquiries in this regard.

PROSECUTOR: We don't make inquiries. But couldn't you concede the possibility that she was desirous of meeting you in order to be rewarded for the information she had given you?

MARGOLIN: I must repeat that had she counted on some pecuniary reward from me, I had no intention of making her an offer. However, as I had indicated to Brazul, if she had come forward with material information about the murder, she would have been compensated.

SHMAKOV: Why did you make a secret of your trip to Kharkov?

MARGOLIN: There was no secret; yet inasmuch as the meeting with Cheberyak had produced no new information, I saw no reason to share my Kharkov experiences with the investigating authorities.

PRESIDING JUDGE: When you met with Cheberyak, did you tell her that if she were to take responsibility for the murder, she would receive 40,000 rubles?

MARGOLIN: This could have been proposed only by one who had taken leave of his senses.

SHMAKOV: Let me repeat: did you or didn't you make that offer?

MARGOLIN: I did not. And may I add that there is nothing in the record to suggest that my mental faculties had been severely impaired.

SHMAKOV: So, there wasn't any reference to money?

MARGOLIN: No, there was not.

ZAMISLOVSKI: I gather from your testimony that those present at the meeting were you, an attorney and leading community leader . . .

MARGOLIN: This sounds like a testimonial . . .

ZAMISLOVSKI: You said so . . .

MARGOLIN: Yes—my being an attorney—that's a fact, but as to whether I'm a "leading community leader," that's your interpretation.

ZAMISLOVSKI: Well, if any reference to your status displeases you, let's just say one who is involved in community affairs, then the Cheberyak woman—with underworld connections—the progressive journalist Brazul-Brushkovsky, and the detective Vygranov. As a rule, such a colorful assortment of people one does not find in conventional social circles.

MARGOLIN: Circumstances make strange bedfellows.

ZAMISLOVSKI: And as to Vygranov, Brazul described him to you as a student?

MARGOLIN: Yes, that's the way he referred to him.

ZAMISLOVSKI: You said that Brazul was a sincere, trustworthy person engaged in quixotic activities . . .

MARGOLIN: Yes, in the best sense of that term.

ZAMISLOVSKI: Yet he deceived you in referring to Vygranov as a student . . .

The testimony of Baruch Zaitsev, grandson of the millionaire Jonas Zaitsev, was significant in two respects:

a) It revealed the work pattern at the brick factory, of which Beilis was the dispatcher, and of the charitable institutions—the chapel and the poorhouse—built on the premises of the Zaitsev estate and sustained by the proceeds of the brick factory, and

b) it showed the religious schism between the late Jonas Zaitsev, a religious Jew, and Baruch Zaitsev, the grandson, who—in his testimony—dismissed Jewish religious practices and beliefs as anachronistic and incompatible with modernity.

This evoked a sharp verbal rebuke from Oscar Gruzenberg, head of the Beilis defense team and a man steeped in Russian and Western culture, but a proud Jew, who upbraided the young Zaitsev for his apologetic and demeaning attitude toward Jewish religious knowledge and tradition.

Gruzenberg's stern "lecture" to young Zaitsev was ruled impermissible and out of order by the Presiding Judge.

Testimony of Baruch Zaitsev
September 30, 1913

PRESIDING JUDGE: What do you know about the case?

BARUCH ZAITSEV: (Silent)

PROSECUTOR: Your name is Baruch?

ZAITSEV: Yes.

PROSECUTOR: Are you the grandson of Jonas Zaitsev, who owned this estate?

ZAITSEV: Yes.

PROSECUTOR: How long ago did he die?

ZAITSEV: Some eight years ago.

PROSECUTOR: Who owns the estate now?

ZAITSEV: The surgical clinic. A poorhouse is also being built there.

PROSECUTOR: You probably know that the poorhouse included a dining hall, which was later converted into a chapel. How did that come about?

ZAITSEV: The rationale was, that if we obtained the necessary permit, the place would be a chapel; if not, it would remain a dining hall. That's the way it turned out.

PROSECUTOR: But the plans projected a dining hall?

ZAITSEV: Yes.

PROSECUTOR: Is Mark Zaitsev Jonas Zaitsev's son? I take it that he and the elder Zaitsev were in charge of the factory. Whom did Mark marry?

ZAITSEV: His wife's maiden name is Ettinger.

PROSECUTOR: Did the Ettingers ever visit Kiev?

ZAITSEV: Yes, his wife's brother visited.

PROSECUTOR: Is this an aristocratic Hebrew family?

ZAITSEV: Yes, it is an aristocratic family.

PROSECUTOR: Where do the Ettingers reside?

ZAITSEV: In Galicia.

PROSECUTOR: Are you aware when Yushchinsky's murder took place?

ZAITSEV: Not precisely. I believe it was on the twelfth of March.

PROSECUTOR: Do you recall, how long before that did Ettinger visit Kiev?

ZAITSEV: I think he was here in January.

PROSECUTOR: Who is he?

ZAITSEV: The brother, Jacob.

PROSECUTOR: Does he have a doctorate in philosophy?

ZAITSEV: No, in chemistry.

PROSECUTOR: Are there any rabbis among the Ettingers?

ZAITSEV: I really don't know, as they always lived abroad.

PROSECUTOR: Shifra, Zaitsev's daughter, is she married to a Landau? Is Landau also a prominent family?

ZAITSEV: Yes, it's a well-known family.

PROSECUTOR: Are there any *tzadiks* or rabbis among them?

ZAITSEV: It could be.

PROSECUTOR: What are your duties on the estate?

ZAITSEV: I am on the management committee of the brick factory, the income of which maintains the clinic.

PROSECUTOR: Do you know Beilis?

ZAITSEV: Certainly. He served when I was in charge.

PROSECUTOR: Do you know what duties he performed for the elder Zaitsev?

ZAITSEV: He was employed there, so he probably did.

PROSECUTOR: No, I'm referring to religious chores. Did he oversee the baking of matzos for members of the family?

ZAITSEV: I didn't know about it until recently.

PROSECUTOR: Was your grandfather very religious?

ZAITSEV: Yes.

PROSECUTOR: Did he belong to the hasidic sect?

ZAITSEV: No, he comes from a family of merchants.

PROSECUTOR: So what?

ZAITSEV: What is your conception of a *hasid*? A religious person? Or you have something else in mind?

PROSECUTOR: My understanding is, that in terms of religion, all Jews are divided into *hasidim* and *mitnagdim*.

ZAITSEV: *Hasid* is one who habitually visits a *tzadik*, but my grandfather, having lived in Kiev for forty years, never traveled anywhere.

PROSECUTOR: Could you tell me where the nearest *tzadik* lives? Is it far from Kiev?

ZAITSEV: I can't tell you. I don't know.

PROSECUTOR: Perhaps my questions are out of place, since I know very little about Jewish customs and mores. It occurs to me that every Jew ought to know whether he is a *hasid* or a *mitnaged*?

ZAITSEV: This question was of no interest to me, nor did it matter to me where the *tzadik* lived.

PROSECUTOR: But the masses, the uneducated Jews, do they belong to the *hasidim* or *mitnagdim*?

ZAITSEV: I don't know.

PROSECUTOR: You know that the Greek Orthodox have different religious wings. The Jews don't have them?

ZAITSEV: We don't have it. We are totally disinterested in the *hasidim*; the Jewish intelligentsia pays no attention to all this.

PROSECUTOR: But surely they know the existence of different denominations?

ZAITSEV: They do, indeed.

PROSECUTOR: You don't know even one *tzadik*?

ZAITSEV: I never saw one.

PROSECUTOR: And you were never interested in these matters?

ZAITSEV: No, I never was.

PROSECUTOR: Tell me, how do you explain the fact that what was built was a poorhouse or a clinic, still a chapel was somehow added to the structure?

ZAITSEV: A chapel was initially projected.

PROSECUTOR: So the plan was to build a fairly large facility?

ZAITSEV: Yes, it turned out to be a very beautiful building, which housed not only a poorhouse; on the main floor was the poorhouse and upstairs the clinic, a very imposing structure.

PROSECUTOR: Were you present at the dedication?

ZAITSEV: I was.

PROSECUTOR: Were any Russians invited, representing the administration?

ZAITSEV: Many were invited; unfortunately, only a very few honored us with their presence.

PROSECUTOR: Who was there, and what transpired?

ZAITSEV: There was a religious service and an unveiling.

PROSECUTOR: And many people were invited?

ZAITSEV: Many Christians were invited, but few showed up.

PROSECUTOR: Was Beilis there?

ZAITSEV: I don't recall.

PROSECUTOR: Was there an elaborate religious ceremony?

ZAITSEV: There was a memorial service for Yonah Zaitsev.

PROSECUTOR: Do you know all the people employed at the factory?

ZAITSEV: Yes.

PROSECUTOR: Did you spend any time at the factory?

ZAITSEV: I did. I knew that Dubovik was manager.

PROSECUTOR: And who were his assistants?

ZAITSEV: There was Beilis and Chernobilski.

PROSECUTOR: You said the unveiling took place on March 7. When did the construction start?

ZAITSEV: I think, at the end of March.

SHMAKOV: You said that a *hasid* was one who was obliged to visit a *tzadik*. Now, the Moslem is duty bound to visit Mecca; was this a similar requirement placed upon a *hasid*?

ZAITSEV: I am not conversant with this question. I suppose if one is a *hasid*, he is required to visit a *tzadik*.

SHMAKOV: Did you know that Beilis's father was a *hasid*?

ZAITSEV: I never met his father and know nothing about him.

SHMAKOV: You did not deny that Beilis—on instructions from your grandfather—traveled to distribute matzos?

ZAITSEV: No, I didn't deny it.

SHMAKOV: And the fact that Beilis's father was a *hasid*?

ZAITSEV: I neither deny nor confirm it, since I knew nothing about him.

PRESIDING JUDGE: The witness doesn't know the father. If you wish, I can direct that question to Beilis.

SHMAKOV: Tell me, are there many people living in the poorhouse?

ZAITSEV: I was not concerned with the poorhouse and know nothing about it.

SHMAKOV: But you are its manager?

ZAITSEV: No, I manage the brick factory.

SHMAKOV: So you have so little interest in the poorhouse that you don't even know how many people stay there?

ZAITSEV: I don't know.

GRUZENBERG: Tell me, you reported that on March seventh there was an unveiling and that invitations were sent to many Christians, but—much to your regret—only a few were present?

ZAITSEV: Yes, only a few.

GRUZENBERG: You sent written invitations to the administration also?

ZAITSEV: We even visited their offices to extend personal invitations.

GRUZENBERG: Few or many, but some Christians did show up?

ZAITSEV: Yes, they did.

GRUZENBERG: Can you name some of those who were present?

ZAITSEV: If I'm not mistaken, Ornazky was there.

GRUZENBERG: Who is he?

ZAITSEV: A medical inspector. There were a few other Christian doctors.

GRUZENBERG: And the religious service was conducted in their presence?

ZAITSEV: Yes.

GRUZENBERG: You were questioned here about the clinic, the poorhouse, etc., that your grandfather left a will stipulating that the brick factory belonging to him should be operated for the benefit of the poorhouse and clinic, that is, that its proceeds be used for charitable purposes?

ZAITSEV: Not for the poorhouse. The poorhouse was erected by his children to perpetuate his memory.

GRUZENBERG: In what manner was the income to be allocated?

ZAITSEV: It was agreed that in conformity with his will, half of the proceeds should be earmarked for the maintenance of the clinic, and half for the poorhouse.

GRUZENBERG: Is the clinic open to Christians?

ZAITSEV: Yes, it provides services to Christians.

GRUZENBERG: If you know, tell us, if you don't, I wish you'd rather not—do Christians come to the clinic?

ZAITSEV: They do.

GRUZENBERG: And they are offered assistance?

ZAITSEV: Yes.

GRUZENBERG: You were questioned about *hasidim* and *tzadiks*, and you replied that as an educated man, you are not a believer. Do six million Jews disavow their religious beliefs? They believe and attend synagogues and pray to God . . .

PRESIDING JUDGE: Mr. Defender, you don't lecture, but ask questions.

GRUZENBERG: That's what I'm doing. Are you suggesting that six million Jews don't pray, don't believe, don't attend services, do not study religious books?

ZAITSEV: They pray, they believe, they read books.

GRUZENBERG: And they are not ashamed to affirm their beliefs loud and clear, but you are ashamed . . .

PRESIDING JUDGE: Mr. Defender, is it permissible to castigate a witness? I must caution you. I told the jury we will present these questions to the experts. And if Mr. Zaitsev did not choose to respond, does he deserve a rebuke? Under the circumstances, you do not have that right.

GRUZENBERG: I accept your reprimand, your honor, and ask that you enter my words into the record.

Feivel Shneerson, an obscure dealer in hay and oats, was summoned as a witness in the trial because he took his meals at Beilis's home, but primarily on account of his name. His name was that of an illustrious rabbinic family—Shneerson (originally Shneor Zalman)—which founded the Lubavich (also known as Chabad) branch of Hasidism. Feivel Shneerson was questioned in court about his religious affiliation. He had none, nor was he aware that he bore a famous name. His testimony demolished the prosecution's claim that a *hasid* was involved in the "ritual murder" rites associated with the Yushchinsky murder.

Testimony of Feivel (Pavel) Shneerson
October 1, 1913

PRESIDING JUDGE: What do you know about this case?

WITNESS: I know nothing about it.

PROSECUTOR: What's your name?

WITNESS: Feivel Shneerson.

PROSECUTOR: What does your father do?

WITNESS: He is a *shohet*—slaughterer.

PROSECUTOR: What is your occupation?

WITNESS: I had a store selling oats and hay.

PROSECUTOR: Did you take your meals at Beilis's place?

WITNESS: Yes.

PROSECUTOR: Did you have the right of residence?

WITNESS: Yes.

PROSECUTOR: Did you know that in Lubavich lives a relative of yours, or namesake, Zalman Shneerson, who was one of the most famous *tzadiks*?

WITNESS: No, I didn't.

SHMAKOV: Do you know Hebrew?

WITNESS: No, I don't.

Testimony of Dobzansky
September 26, 1913

Dobzansky, a bar owner, offered a thumbnail characterization of Vera Cheberyak and her criminal associates.

GRUZENBERG: Do you know Vera Cheberyak?

WITNESS: I sure do. I know her very well, as she used to frequent my tavern in the company of some shady characters.

GRUZENBERG: What's your opinion of her?

WITNESS: She is the lowest of the lowest. Her home is a den where all kinds of shady transactions were made. It was also a depository of stolen goods. Indeed I know her mighty well.

ZAMISLOVSKI: You said Vera Cheberyak used to come to your bar in the company of some shady types?

WITNESS: Yes.

ZAMISLOVSKI: That this was a group of unsavory characters—do you know it now, or you knew it then?

WITNESS: No—this was known to everyone then.

ZAMISLOVSKI: What do you mean by "shady types"?

WITNESS: Simply put, these were persons engaged in thievery.

ZAMISLOVSKI: You and everyone around knew about it?

WITNESS: Yes.

ZAMISLOVSKI: And the police knew?

WITNESS: Yes, the police knew.

ZAMISLOVSKI: How did they come dressed?

WITNESS: They were dressed in a variety of uniforms.

ZAMISLOVSKI: And you recognized them in spite of the uniforms?

WITNESS: I knew every one of them.

PROSECUTOR: Did you know Shneerson?

WITNESS: Yes, he was my neighbor. I used to buy hay from him.

PROSECUTOR: Did he have the right of residence?

WITNESS: He told me that he did.

PROSECUTOR: So you know it because he told you so?

SHMAKOV: Tell me. Is Shneerson dark complexioned?

WITNESS: Yes. He is black.

SHMAKOV: Do you know where he took his meals?

WITNESS: At Beilis's home.

SHMAKOV: Did he ever tell you that he hails from a prominent Jewish family?

WITNESS: No, he never did.

SHMAKOV: Did he ever mention that he is a *tzadik* or that he lives with one?

WITNESS: No.

GRUZENBERG: Tell me please, this same Shneerson you referred to, who had a small store in which he sold hay and oats. Wasn't he a soldier, and didn't he complete his military service?

WITNESS: Yes, he was. He's a young man.

KARABCHEVSKY: Do you know what is meant by *tzadik*?

WITNESS: Yes.

KARABCHEVSKY: What about Beilis? Is he also a veteran?

WITNESS: Yes.

KARABCHEVSKY: Did he see military service?

WITNESS: Yes, he did.

ZARUDNY: I respectfully request to put in the record that the prosecutor asked the witness whether the witness's neighbor, Shneerson, had a trade permit. This question was posed by the prosecutor, consequently it calls for our consideration. Does a certain Shneerson have a right to trade in hay? Secondly . . . Interrupted by Presiding Judge: The prosecutor referred to a residence permit, not a trade permit.

ZARUDNY: I apologize for my inexactitude. Did he have a right to live?

PROSECUTOR: I did not say did he have a right to live. I said, did he have a residential permit?

ZARUDNY: That is correct. It is precisely about his right of domicile that I am speaking. I hope you do not have any doubts that a Jew has a right to live, or perhaps you sometimes question that right, too.

PRESIDING JUDGE: I will ask you, Mr. Defender, not to divert our attention in so serious a case. Your remarks will be put into the record.

SHMAKOV: Every time I speak about a Jew, Mr. Zarudny asks that it be put into the record. Pretty soon the record will be bulging with Jews.

4

The Broken Record
"That's What Zhenya Said."

If the Beilis trial were to be showcased as a courtroom drama, the lead role would be undoubtedly assigned not to Beilis, but to a rotund, middle-aged woman named Vera Cheberyak, popularly known in her neighborhood as Vera "Sibiriak," a reference to her association with criminal elements who were frequently banished to Siberia. Pugnacious and vindictive with those who dared to cross her, she could squelch a critic with a torrent of invective that would make a drill sergeant wince. There was, however, another side to Vera Cheberyak. She was attracted to younger men, and one of her lovers was a Frenchman, Pavel Miffle, age 19, whom she helped occasionally with small sums of money and food. In a fit of jealousy, she blinded him by throwing sulfuric acid in his face and he, in turn, gave her a merciless beating, forcing her to go around for weeks with a bandaged head. In the course of her frequent encounters with Brazul-Brushkovsky and various police functionaries, she attempted to place the blame for Yushchinsky's murder on her French paramour. Her home served as a hangout for Kiev's most notorious outlaws, for whom she acted as a counselor, hostess, procuress, and fence. Her husband, Vassily, a postal clerk, was too timid and submissive to object to his domineering wife's extracurricular activities. He slept in a separate room, kept to himself, and was rarely, if ever, admitted into the salon, where his wife held sway. The Russian writer Korolenko, an observer at the trial, referred to her as a "woman of striking character" and a New York *Times* correspondent wrote that "Cheberyak continues to be the most striking figure at the trial. She sits with a sphinx-like expression in front of the witness-stand and is never at a loss for an answer when confronted with those who give testimony against her." Another journalist remarked that she was "clever, crafty, knows how to lead people by the nose and how to manipulate the underworld . . . she is without a doubt a genius of a woman, a very rare criminal type."

While the charge that she contrived to poison her son and daughter for fear that they inadvertently might implicate her in the Yushchinsky murder had not been substantiated, it was never totally ruled out. Thus a government agent monitoring the trial wrote: "It is possible that the mother herself poisoned them, a matter which competent persons consider more than likely." In her several appearances at the trial, Vera Cheberyak was treated—by the presiding judge and the prosecution—with a deference designed to accentuate her status as a protected witness. When she stumbled in her zigzagging testimony, the presiding judge came to her rescue, assuring her that "she was under no obligation to respond to questions that may incriminate her." In response to questions by the defense about the many contradictions in her testimony, she relied on one standard answer: "That's what Zhenya told me." Since her son Zhenya was no longer available to corroborate her testimony, having died months before the trial, she felt that she was safe and untouchable. It was reported that some time after the conclusion of the trial, Vera Cheberyak received an invitation from a circus to present a pantomime of the murder, but the local authorities squelched the enterprise.

"All in all," observed writer Maurice Samuel, "Vera Cheberyak was a woman born out of her time and setting. In the Italy of Cesare Borgia and Caterina Sforza she might have found an adequate field for her varied talents."[1]

Testimony of Vera Cheberyak
October 2, 1913

PRESIDING JUDGE: Madam witness, remember, you have taken an oath to testify only to the truth. What do you know about this case?

WITNESS: Please read to me my previous testimony.

PRESIDING JUDGE: You forgot what you testified to?

WITNESS: Can I remember everything?

PRESIDING JUDGE: Testify as to what you do remember. Should we find some contradictions, we will make public your original testimony.

WITNESS: I lived on Upper Yurkovskaya Street, Number forty. This was when Zhenya was five years old, he was too small to walk. When Zhenya was eight years old, he became acquainted with Andrey Yushchinsky. Yushchinsky started visiting us, taking walks with Zhenya. They became very close. I didn't know Andrey's last name. We called him *domovoy* (goblin). When I moved out from there, I never saw Yushchinsky again and don't know whether he came to our home or not, but I do know that they recently did take a walk. Some eight to nine months after Yushchinsky moved to Slabodka, his body was discovered. As I walked out into the street, I saw a large throng—police, uniformed guards—telling me, "You know the body of a boy was found." I couldn't leave the home

1. Maurice Samuel, *Blood Accusation* (Philadelphia: The Jewish Publication Society, 1966), p. 35.

at that time because my husband was at work. Later, when I did go there, there was a large crowd and no one was permitted into the cave. Soon copybooks and other papers were found and then it was announced that the body was that of Andrey Yushchinsky, a student of the religious school. I ran into Dobzansky and he said, "Sure, it's Andrey Yushchinsky." And I said, "It couldn't be." I called my son to view the body, and he said, "Yes, Mama, it is Andrey." I was asked how long ago was he at your place and I said since he moved to Slabodka, I haven't seen him. Zhenya said that some two weeks ago he visited our home, I can't remember precisely, but perhaps it was the last day when he asked me to take a stroll with him. The next time I went to the cave, Andrey's mother was there. I said, "Was this your boy?" and she said, "Yes, it's mine," but she didn't cry. I said to her, "You have sustained a terrible loss," and she said, "I had a premonition that he'll end up like this." I said, "Did you watch over him?" and she answered casually, "I didn't watch." Then came Fedor Nezhinsky. I said, "How did it happen?" and he said, "It's all very clear to us. We'll eventually find out the truth. It's all for money." Several days later, I went with my three children to the funeral. Many people were there, and when Andrey was buried, leaflets were thrown. I thought these must be students throwing pieces of paper in the grave but as it turned out, these were leaflets. Zhenya picked one up. It had some writings in a blue pencil. Polishchuk or someone else took the leaflet away from Zhenya, so he could not see what was written in it. Several days after the funeral, Zhenya and I were summoned for a hearing. They kept asking me, "Remember when Andrey visited you." I said, "I haven't seen him for a year," but Zhenya said he did come to see us. Then they questioned Zhenya—"When was that?" Zhenya said he couldn't remember—some two, three weeks ago. I've been questioned several times thereafter. Subsequently, when the Malitsky woman reported to the authorities that Andrey was killed in my flat, I was arrested and they questioned me again and Zhenya. When I was arrested, Zhenya with my husband remained home with my two girls. Around eleven o'clock when my husband was still at work, Zhenya went for a walk with his friends. Two girlfriends came to visit my daughters, another little boy came over to see Zhenya. When they escorted the girls home, a man walked over to them. They said it was a Jew, and two others stood nearby. The man asked, "Are you Zhenya Cheberyak?" He answered yes. "Where was Andrey killed?" they asked. It was between ten and eleven at night. The man took Zhenya's hand, but he tore himself free and rushed up the stairs. The next day Krasovsky and Vygranov came by and said, "Your boy must be shown the cave." I asked Zhenya, "Can you recall if someone chased Andrey?" He pondered and remembered. Yes, he said, there was such an incident! I said, "Tell us about it," and he said, "It was in the morning. Mama went to the market, Papa was at work and we were alone. Andrey came and took me for a walk." They were joined by the two Nakonechny girls and another girl and they all went to the revolving clay mixer within the factory grounds. Zhenya said when they sat down—he on one side, Andrey on the other—the Beilis boys were also there, and two other boys. They started chasing each other, the boys started throwing stones. At some point, Beilis grabbed Zhenya by one hand and Andrey with the other. Zhenya was slim and dexterous and managed to wiggle out and run away, but Andrey could not. What happened to Andrey I don't remember. This was also what I told the examiner.

PRESIDING JUDGE: Zhenya told you all this?

WITNESS: Yes—me and my husband.

PRESIDING JUDGE: Weren't you asked why you didn't report this incident at that time?

WITNESS: Because the kids have been chased quite often but there never was an incident when they were dragged. When they started questioning Zhenya, he recalled the incident.

PRESIDING JUDGE: Tell us about Brazul.

WITNESS: When Zhenya was called to the examiner, I was still under arrest. When I reported what happened—that Beilis caught Andrey—I was freed. Then Krasovsky arrived and said, "Do you know who I am?" I said no. "I am Krasovsky. I was assigned to investigate this case. I know that most of the data is already in, hence I am releasing you, but on one condition: you've got to leave your flat and stay inside. Don't get in my way!" I said, "I can't leave before the twentieth, as I have no money." He said, "I'll advance you the money." We moved out into another flat. Within a few days, I was arrested again and spent seventeen days at the Boulevard Precinct. I was interrogated by magistrate Fenenko. When they let me go, Zhenya was in the hospital. My two girls were in bed, also sick. I went to the hospital and found Zhenya unconscious. The doctor said, "He has dysentery." I said, "Is there any hope?" The doctor said, "Don't expect anything good." I said, "Well, will you permit me to take him home?" and the doctor said, "Go ahead—he's not likely to survive, anyway." I said, "Let him die on my hands." I took him home, and the boy died, never uttering a word. Two weeks later Valya also died and Luda was still ill. Sometime later Krasovsky appeared and said, "Vera Vladimirovna, your children were poisoned." I couldn't believe it.

On a second or third visit he kept insisting, "Your kids were poisoned. Whom do you suspect?" Then Brazul showed up with a new refrain: "Vera, you must help us. You were unlawfully detained, your children were poisoned, and you as a mother must take revenge."

"How can I help you?" I said. "You have to help us, otherwise your husband will lose his job and you'll be in dire need." On another visit he told me, "Your husband will be dismissed on November seventh unless you help us. I'll take you to see a highly influential gentleman who will unravel the whole thing—why your kids were poisoned, why you are being constantly arrested." He came again on December sixth and proposed that I travel with him to Kharkov. I agreed. We went to Kharkov and stopped at an expensive inn. Once I said yes, Brazul answered that my husband will again have a job. We took the express train to Kharkov. Once there, we went to see the "influential person," a distinguished-looking man whom Brazul introduced as a member of the Imperial Duma from St. Petersburg. He said, "Tell me how it was. How were you arrested?" I started telling him when, where, and how, and he said, "What you're telling me I already know. Tell me how Zhenya died." I told him and then touched on the Beilis episode. He stopped me, saying, "Don't talk about Beilis. You repeat what I am telling you, namely that criminal elements are involved. Your son was deceived. He was told to say what he did." I said, "What do you want from me?" "We'll do for you whatever you desire, if only you take responsibility for the case."

Presiding Judge: What case?

Witness: I said, "I don't understand. What should I take upon myself?" and he said, "The murder take upon yourself." I said, "How can a woman murder?" He said, "You only have to agree and we'll take care about the details. Just sign a paper. We'll give you the documents to go abroad where they will never find you." I said, "Why me?" He said, "You're suitable for that role, since Zhenya was Andrey's friend. Everyone has seen Andrey in the company of Zhenya, which makes you right for the part." I said, "So I'll take the blame, but what will be next?" He said, "If you are arrested, the best lawyers will be engaged to defend you. You have nothing to fear." At that point, two other gentlemen entered from the next room whom I had seen previously at a restaurant in Kiev. One of them said, "We'll give you forty thousand and the necessary documents to travel abroad. If you procrastinate signing the paper, it will be too late, as this is the most opportune time." I said, "I'll talk to my husband" and walked out with Brazul and Vygranov.

PROSECUTOR: I'll ask you a few questions, but you have every right to refuse to answer. Was your home frequented by suspicious persons?

WITNESS: Yes. Mendzelevsky used to visit.

PROSECUTOR: Was he tried for theft?

WITNESS: Yes.

PRESIDING JUDGE: Questions that may seem to you incriminating, you have a right to say, "I refuse to answer as provided by law."

PROSECUTOR: When your children started telling you about the incident at the Zaitsev factory, didn't you tell them, "You better keep quiet, don't blab"?

WITNESS: No, I didn't.

PROSECUTOR: Andrey was found dead in March, but Zhenya told you about Beilis only in June.

WITNESS: Yes.

KARABCHEVSKY: The witness seems to have forgotten a great deal, and there are contradictions with previous testimony. I therefore request that the previous testimony be made public.

PRESIDING JUDGE: Petition of the defense granted. Witness, we will read part of your previous testimony, and you will explain the contradictions. The witness was questioned June 24, 1911, and said inter alia: "When Yushchinsky's body was found, Zhenya told me that same day, 'You see, Mama, I told you what Fedor said to me about the kikes slaughtering Andrey.' I then questioned Zhenya as to when Andrey visited him the last time. Zhenya replied that Andrey came to him some three weeks before his body was discovered. According to Zhenya, he met Andrey on the street next to our home. He had books strapped under his belt and wore a red shirt and black jacket. He had no coat. The meeting took place around 3:00 P.M. Andrey asked Zhenya to go for a walk with him but Zhenya declined. That's all Zhenya told me."

PRESIDING JUDGE: You see, this is what you testified to on the twenty-fourth of June, 1911. Why did you change your testimony? You said Zhenya met Andrey on the street and that it was at 2:00 P.M."

WITNESS: That's what Zhenya told me.

PRESIDING JUDGE: The witness was also questioned on April 22, 1911, and declared, inter alia: "When Andrey moved to Slabodka, I haven't seen him since, and if he moved in May of last year, that would mean that I haven't seen him for almost a year, but my son Zhenya told me that some four weeks before his body was discovered Andrey came over and called him out into the street, suggesting that they go for a walk to the Zaitsev enclave where he was subsequently found dead. I wasn't home at the time, and Zhenya did not want to leave the flat unlocked and therefore he didn't go with him. Thus Andrey went to the Zaitsev estate by himself. According to Zhenya, it was approximately 2:00 P.M. However, Zhenya didn't tell me about this at the time and revealed this incident after Andrey's body was discovered. I recall asking Zhenya did Andrey come around to Lukyanovka at any time since his parents moved, and Zhenya said that shortly after they relocated, Andrey came over several times and he and Zhenya took walks, but that it was in the fall of last year."

GRUZENBERG: When you were questioned for the first time, you testified that Zhenya related to you as follows: "When Andrey relocated to Slabodka, I haven't seen him since."

PRESIDING JUDGE: This was your first testimony. Will you clarify for us why you testified as you did? In your second interrogation in April, you testified differently.

WITNESS: Because this is what Zhenya told me.

PRESIDING JUDGE: You better tell the truth. Remember, you're under oath.

WITNESS: I remember, but that's what Zhenya told me.

GRUZENBERG: I would request that her four other depositions not be read, but that you acknowledge that prior to her testimony on July 10, 1912, that is, before Brazul entered a complaint against her to the police authorities, in which she was directly accused of the murder, she said that Andrey came over and suggested that they go for a walk, but her son did not go.

Vassily Cheberyak, Vera's husband, repeated what he had allegedly learned from his son, Zhenya, to wit, that Andrey, Zhenya, and other children were playing on the Zaitsev estate near the brick factory, that Beilis chased them and grabbed Andrey and Zhenya; Zhenya managed to break loose, but Andrey did not; that Ludmilla Cheberyak had seen Andrey being dragged by Beilis and other Jews, "who looked like *tzadiks*," toward the factory kiln.

Testimony of Vassily Cheberyak

WITNESS: I was home. Suddenly Zhenya appeared at the door, very pale. I asked, "What's wrong?" He said they were all playing on the factory grounds when the kike Mendel and two others started chasing them and grabbed Zhenya and Andrey. My son managed to tear himself away and escape. What happened to Andrey I don't know.

PRESIDING JUDGE: This is what your son told you. When did he tell you this?

WITNESS: The same day. All my children were playing on the factory grounds, also two other girls, also the youngest one, who was weaker than the others and thus stayed behind the others. She saw Mendel dragging Andrey toward the kiln.

PRESIDING JUDGE: Who saw this?

WITNESS: My youngest daughter and son.

PRESIDING JUDGE: And your son told you this?

WITNESS: Yes.

PRESIDING JUDGE: How much time elapsed from this incident to the disappearance of Andrey? Was it before or after the homicide?

WITNESS: No, this was before the homicide.

PRESIDING JUDGE: Are you employed in the postal telegraph office?

WITNESS: Yes.

PRESIDING JUDGE: You were home at the time?

WITNESS: Yes.

PRESIDING JUDGE: Was it in the morning around noon, or evening?

WITNESS: This was in the morning. It was a sunny bright day.

PRESIDING JUDGE: So he came running and told you about this incident that Beilis grabbed Andrey?

WITNESS: Beilis and two other "kikes" who by his description looked like rabbis or *tzadiks*. He said they didn't look like the ones he usually saw on the street, but new faces.

PRESIDING JUDGE: Didn't he tell you that Beilis's son was also there?

WITNESS: Beilis's family was there.

PRESIDING JUDGE: Did you attach importance to this incident?

WITNESS: Yes, I did, because there were previous instances when Jews grabbed Christian children.

PRESIDING JUDGE: You took particular note of this right away when Zhenya told you, or when the body was discovered?

WITNESS: I warned him not to venture into the Zaitsev grounds. I ordered him not to.

PRESIDING JUDGE: Why didn't you report this to the authorities when the body was discovered?

WITNESS: At that time the discovery of the body was not yet announced.

PRESIDING JUDGE: But afterwards, once the body was found and it became public, why didn't you report to the authorities what Zhenya told you?

WITNESS: For some time I didn't know about the murder.

GRUZENBERG: Please tell me, Mr. Witness, on the date—the twelfth—when you found out that Andrey perished, you said you didn't recall that date?

WITNESS: I didn't know yet on the twelfth.

GRUZENBERG: I understand. I'm asking you on the twelfth, do you recall how long you were on duty on your job?

WITNESS: No, I don't remember.

GRUZENBERG: Do you know that your supervisor advised the court examiner the precise hours you were on duty on that date?

WITNESS: No.

GRUZENBERG: Perhaps you remember that on the twelfth you were on duty from 9:00 A.M. to 3:00 P.M.

WITNESS: I don't remember.

GRUZENBERG: You don't remember? Tell me this, then. What's the walking distance from your home to where you work?

WITNESS: A twenty-five-minute walk.

GRUZENBERG: Now let me ask you. When Zhenya came running and told you that Beilis and two Jewish rabbis or religious tutors, as you reported, pounced on Andrey and dragged him, did you subsequently ask Zhenya whether Andrey visited him on that day?

WITNESS: I asked him.

GRUZENBERG: And what was his answer?

WITNESS: He said that he didn't, but called him out.

GRUZENBERG: Is that what your son told you? That's what you reported to the examiner?

WITNESS: Yes.

GRUZENBERG: I'd like to verify with the examiner whether that's what you really testified to. Now tell me, please, I'm sure you know that your wife has been constantly badgered by detectives. That she was six times summoned to appear before the court examiner. Didn't you tell her, "Why don't you tell them how it was, that one Jew grabbed and dragged Andrey?" Did you tell her that?

WITNESS: No, I didn't tell her.

GRUZENBERG: Why not?

WITNESS: This is what Zhenya told us.

GRUZENBERG: Let me repeat my question. You testified before the magistrate on December 20, 1911. Until that date your wife was persistently pestered by detectives—was called six times for hearings before the examiner. Didn't you tell her, "Why don't you come clean before the authorities? Tell them about the Jews enticing and seizing the boy and the boy was lost."

WITNESS: (Silent)

PRESIDING JUDGE: Why didn't you speak up?

WITNESS: I didn't tell her because she knew it herself.

GRUZENBERG: Come now. Jews seizing a Christian boy and causing his death. Why didn't you report such a monstrous Jewish barbarity?

WITNESS: I didn't pay attention.

GRUZENBERG: I respectfully ask the court to make public records relevant to his previous testimony. Also the information elicited from the telegraph office indicating when he was on duty.

PRESIDING JUDGE: Petition granted.

MEMBER OF THE COURT (reading the testimony): Vassily Cheberyak, having been examined by the magistrate on December 20, 1911, declared inter alia: "Some time in the summer of this year, when we still occupied the old premises adjacent to the Zaitsev factory, around 11 o'clock at night, Zhenya, who was playing with other kids on the street near our home, burst into the home in a state of alarm and told me that minutes before some Jew approached him asking him to lead him to the cave where Yushchinsky's body was discovered. Zhenya refused and wanted to walk away, whereupon the Jew grabbed his hand forcefully to detain him. Zhenya broke loose and ran home with the Jew following until he reached our home, but he was pounced upon by our dogs and was forced to leave." On December 20, 1911, Cheberyak testified that a short time prior to the discovery of the body, approximately three to four days before that, "Zhenya rushed into the house breathlessly and told me that together with Yushchinsky he played on the

Zaitsev factory grounds where Beilis saw him. The latter
chased him, while Beilis's children laughed. Where Andrey
ran, I don't know, and I didn't ask Zhenya about that. This
incident occurred in the morning around 11:00 A.M., and I
remember clearly warning Zhenya he shouldn't dare to play
on the factory grounds hereafter. I don't recall the exact date,
but repeat that it was several days before the body was found.
In reply to a question by the prosecutor as to the precise date
of this incident, I answered that it might have been more than
three to four days before the body was found, perhaps a week
or so, and it might have been around dinner time—around 3
o'clock. What I do remember clearly is that it was light outside." (The court reveals the periods the witness was on duty at
the telegraph office).

GRUZENBERG: You heard what you testified to before. Yesterday you said that Zhenya had told you that when they
played on the Zaitsev estate they were attacked by Beilis and
two other rabbis and they dragged Andrey. Not a word about
the rabbis, nor did you say that he was dragged. You said
where Andrey ran to, you don't know.

WITNESS: I refreshed my memory.

GRUZENBERG: When you talked to the examiner Zhenya was
already dead. Didn't he pass away on August eighth?

WITNESS: Yes.

GRUZENBERG: You testified in December, hence you couldn't
have had additional information from Zhenya.

WITNESS: (Silent)

The priest Sinkevich was called to give communion to the dying
boy, Zhenya Cheberyak. The priest was the head of the monarchist
Double-Headed Eagle organization in Kiev and a prime mover in
the effort to implicate Jews in the Yushchinsky murder and shelter
Vera Cheberyak from prosecution. Always fearful that her son, who
had been delirious most of the time, might say something that would
tie her to the murder, Vera Cheberyak had gone out of her way to

secure the services of the anti-Semitic priest whose organization was pledged to keep her out of trouble. The boy was in agony, whispering to the priest, "Father, Father . . ." while his mother was facing him when he died.

Testimony of the Priest Sinkevich

WITNESS: I was called to give communion to the sick boy Zhenya Cheberyak. As I was preparing to leave, the boy called to me, "Father, Father." I was deeply moved, walked over to him, and asked him, "What is it, my child?" He didn't answer but whispered again, "Father, Father." I again asked him, "What is it, my child?" But as much as I tried to encourage him to speak, he was silent.

PRESIDING JUDGE: The boy was very ill?

WITNESS: Yes, he was dying.

PRESIDING JUDGE: Was he conscious?

WITNESS: I suppose he was, since he said "Father."

SHMAKOV: When you heard him calling you "Father," what did you observe? Did you sense an inner struggle?

WITNESS: I thought he wanted to say something but hesitated. He seemed to be tormented.

SHMAKOV: How do you explain that?

WITNESS: I'm at a loss to explain.

SHMAKOV: Where was Vera Cheberyak at that time?

WITNESS: She was in the same room.

SHMAKOV: Was she behind you?

WITNESS: Yes.

SHMAKOV: Was she facing the boy?

WITNESS: Most likely, yes.

SHMAKOV: What was she doing? You didn't see?

WITNESS: I didn't see. Everyone was discussing the Beilis case, and I suppose she was trying to let him know.

PRESIDING JUDGE: You presume but you didn't see?

WITNESS: Yes. It was my supposition.

GRIGOREVICH-BARSKY: On your previous visits did you have any conversation with Vera Cheberyak about the Yushchinsky murder?

WITNESS: As I recall, there was such conversation.

GRIGOREVICH-BARSKY: What did she tell you?

WITNESS: I don't remember precisely. I recall her saying the Jews are being accused in vain.

5

Bruised but Unbowed

The Russian Sherlock Holmes

The ineptitude of the Kiev investigators and detectives had been scorned and ridiculed by both the defense and prosecution teams throughout the trial proceedings. One detective, however, Nikolai Krasovsky, stood out as a model of unquestioned ability and ingenuity. Krasovsky had acquired a national reputation, having solved several complicated crimes, and was popularly known as Russia's Sherlock Holmes. Krasovsky was not eager to accept the assignment of directing the investigation into the Yushchinsky murder. He said that "I knew from previous experience what to expect; intrigues, unpleasantness, but I was told not to worry since the czar himself was interested in the case." To protect him against internal skulduggery, he was placed with the gendarmery instead of the regular police.

However, if the Kiev administration thought that Krasovsky would toe the line charted by the official hierarchy, it soon had reason to rue his appointment. Krasovsky had professional pride and integrity, but he knew that his predecessor, Mishchuk, was relieved of his command because he ran afoul of the meddlesome but highly influential student Golubev, a leading member of the Double-Headed Eagle and of the Union of the Russian People. To keep Golubev off his back, Krasovsky told him that he did not rule out the possibility that fanatical Jews may have had a hand in the murder.

In his testimony, Krasovsky maintained that he had never doubted that Cheberyak and her crowd were the perpetrators of the crime, dismissing the ritual-murder version propounded by Golubev as sheer nonsense. When it became apparent that Krasovsky's investigation was focused on Cheberyak and her associates, and not on Beilis, the word was out that Krasovsky was becoming expendable. When Krasovsky was authorized to order Vera Cheberyak's arrest, the Kiev conspirators (Golubev, Chaplinsky, etc.) demanded his scalp, and before long he was removed from the Yushchinsky case and banished to serve as head of the rural police. That reassignment did not appease Golubev and the Union of the Russian People, who felt that Krasovsky was let off too easily; thus after a respite of four months, Krasovsky was dismissed from government service.

Embittered and humiliated by his dismissal, Krasovsky was determined to vindicate himself and reenter the case as a private investigator. Soon after he reappeared in his newly assumed role, he was summoned by the investigating magistrate to explain what he was up to.

Krasovsky did not mince words: "Owing to the interference of the rightist organization, this case could not develop along normal lines. The rightist organization think that this is a ritual murder, and I am convinced that this is an ordinary murder committed by ordinary criminals from motives of revenge." Four days later, Krasovsky was arrested on a charge of embezzling—nine years earlier—the sum of sixteen kopeks (eight cents) from a prisoner in his custody. He was jailed for six weeks and finally acquitted. Undeterred by what he perceived to be officially inspired harassment, the detective resumed his investigation with renewed vigor.

Krasovsky's testimony at the trial brought out the extraordinary tenacity and incorruptibility of this able investigator, who—in the face of a relentless cross-examination by the prosecution—stood his ground and emerged unscathed as one of the unsung heroes of the Beilis trial.

Testimony of Nikolai Krasovsky

WITNESS: At the beginning of September 1910, I served as commander of the Kiev secret police. In November I was reassigned to a different region, but on May 4, 1911, I received a telegram which read as follows: "By order of the governor: proceed immediately to Kiev." On arrival in Kiev, I found out that I was summoned not by the governor but by the prosecutor, whom I went to see early on May 5. At the prosecutor's office I saw the former prosecutor of the district court, Brandorf, prosecutor Chaplinsky, and the director of the department of police, Liadov. The prosecutor explained that I was summoned in connection with the Yushchinsky murder, specifically as a specialist in detective work. He told me to carry on my investigation independently and call on the investigator and the prosecutor should I need assistance. I was also told that in order to conceal my official involvement in the case, the authorities would be advised that I was officially on leave, that my presence in Kiev was necessitated by personal business, since I owned some property in that town.

This masquerade was not entirely successful, as I was well known in Kiev in police circles and my co-workers immediately suspected that my stay was officially sanctioned. I was briefed about the status of the investigation by the magistrate Fenenko, but his briefing failed to indicate either the reasons, motives, or character of the crime. I soon realized that a major oversight in the investigation to date stemmed from the failure to examine the site where the murdered boy was found. I then proceeded to thoroughly inspect the cave, the adjoining areas, including the grounds of the Zaitsev factory, as well as the area where the mother and stepfather of the boy lived. In this I encountered some difficulties, since no one in the prosecutor's office informed the commander of the secret police of my "unofficial" involvement in the investigation.

PRESIDING JUDGE: You're obviously referring to Commander Mishchuk?

WITNESS: Yes, Mishchuk. To assist me I enlisted the services of former agents of the secret police, Polishchuk and Vygranov. In addition, I utilized the assistance of other persons in the expanding investigation. This state of affairs provoked some confusion and embarrassment as officials of the secret police were not told of my assignment, nor was I at liberty to divulge the "conspiratorial" nature of my duties. I complained to the magistrate and the prosecutor, which ultimately resulted in the commander of the secret police being instructed to cease his activities in the Yushchinsky investigation.

As I proceeded making inquiries among the local inhabitants, I immediately noticed a pronounced reluctance to talk about the case and I soon realized that this reluctance stemmed from some extraneous influence. It soon dawned on me that there was a pervasive air of fear of something or someone. Perusing the assembled data, it occurred to me that the crime was committed by a criminal organization or simply a gang of thieves. In the course of the investigation I repeatedly ran into Golubev and Razmitalsky, who had shown a great interest in the case.

At that time rumors were afloat that the murder was the work of Jews for ritual purposes. The above named, who were members of a monarchist organization, kept after me for my assessment of the case. At the same time, every measure I undertook that did not meet with the approval of the monarchists found its expression in the rightist press. I therefore reported to the prosecutor that steps ought to be taken to restrain these meddlers who impeded the investigation. Nevertheless, I did not overlook the Zaitsev estate and the saddlery where various tools, including awls which corresponded with the instruments reportedly used in the murder of Yushchinsky, were on hand. However, I learned that those tools belonged to a former saddler, a Christian, who ordinarily used them in his work. Nevertheless, my investigation invariably led me to the Cheberyak home. When I attempted to interrogate the Cheberyak neighbors, they clammed up. At one point when questioning Shachovsky, he grudgingly revealed that he saw Yushchinsky on the morning of March twelfth, standing by the Cheberyak home with Zhenya Cheberyak and another boy some distance away. Sometime thereafter, I tried to question Zhenya in the presence of his mother and father and on occasion Zhenya alone. This was a stubborn, secretive boy, but streetwise, who constantly evaded my questions. The Cheberyak children gave me the impression of being scared. I learned that Zhenya had a great deal of influence on Yushchinsky who occasionally, instead of going to school, spent time with Zhenya at the Cheberyak home. On my several visits to the Cheberyak home I noticed that the windows in the hallway leading to the Cheberyak flat provided a clear view of the cave where Yushchinsky's body was found. This fact and the bits of pieces of information I elicited from the neighbors reinforced my conviction that Cheberyak was somehow involved in the murder.

With the arrest of Beilis, there was a rash of items in the local press intimating that Jews were involved in the Yushchinsky murder and that the investigation carried on by me and other officials strayed off the right course. Several press items alluded to me personally as having been bribed by Jews to steer the investigation into the wrong channels. Needless to say these rumors dismayed me and made my position untenable.

Simultaneously with those press reports I was subjected to a barrage of barbs and official reprimands from persons associated with me in the investigation. I reported to the magistrate and subsequently to the prosecutor's office that under these circumstances I could not continue with my work. At the same time Mishchuk started accusing me openly of being responsible for his removal from this case, which distressed me deeply. I therefore petitioned the prosecutor's office to relieve me of my duties. As early as August, I requested that someone of the police department be assigned to assist me, specifically recommending Kirichenko for that assignment, since I considered him capable and trustworthy. My request was granted. I knew that Mishchuk enjoyed the confidence of the governor and in view of Mishchuk's antagonism toward me, I knew that my days as investigator were numbered. And, indeed, on December 31, 1911, I was relieved of my official duties.

PROSECUTOR: How were you dismissed?

WITNESS: I considered my dismissal unjust, especially since I compiled a good record of service.

PRESIDING JUDGE: Thus, you felt your dismissal was unfair?

WITNESS: Yes, it was undeserved, and since I felt I was ill-treated on account of the Yushchinsky case, I decided to devote myself exclusively to this case in a private capacity in order to rehabilitate myself. My first objective was to keep a close eye on Vera Cheberyak. My suspicions were reinforced by another incident which I learned from Shachovsky. He confirmed that Zhenya Cheberyak, Yushchinsky, and another boy, while playing near the cave where the body was subsequently found, obtained some switches. Andrey's switch was straighter and more flexible than Zhenya's, whereupon the latter asked Andrey to give him his switch. Andrey refused and the boys quarreled. To intimidate Andrey, Zhenya declared that he would tell Andrey's aunt that he was skipping school, to which Andrey retorted, "If you'll do that, I'll write to the secret police that your mother frequently entertains thieves who bring stolen goods to your home." Zhenya went home and reported the conversation to his mother. I found out that Andrey frequented the Cheberyak home and his presence did not inhibit the thieves from talking freely about their various exploits. The criminals didn't pay too much attention to Andrey, but when police harassment of Cheberyak intensified, I felt sure that Yushchinsky figured in their calculations as to who might be feeding information to the authorities.

My interest in the Cheberyak family led me to establish a contact with the Dyakonov sisters, who had an intimate relationship with Vera Cheberyak. I learned that in the course of the gatherings and parties held at the Cheberyak home by members of the underworld, the "good old days" of 1905 were frequently recalled, at which time, as a result of pogroms against Jews then occurring in Kiev, Cheberyak and her friends greatly benefited from the resultant loot and pillage; in fact, her home became a veritable warehouse of stolen goods.

On March 12, following a police search the previous day at the Cheberyak home, Ekaterina Dyakonov visited the Cheberyaks. The door was locked. She knocked and Vera opened the door and ushered her hurriedly into the kitchen. She noticed a steaming samovar in a second room where Vassily, Vera's husband, usually slept. Several persons, including Singayevsky, Rudzinsky, and Latyshev, sat around the table drinking tea. There was a knock on the door and Vera, unlocking the door, ushered in Yushchinsky, who asked for Zhenya. Vera summoned Zhenya and the two started a conversation about gunpowder, which Yushchinsky wanted for his play gun.

Ekaterina Dyakonov related another incident when Vera Cheberyak came to their home and asked the sisters to spend the night with her, insisting that she was afraid to be alone at night, her husband being away. Ekaterina agreed and they proceeded to the Cheberyak flat. Ekaterina recalled that at night, while accidentally stretching her foot through the bed's

railing, her toes touched an object which seemed like a crate.
She subsequently asked Vera about it and the latter said that it
was "hot clothing," but Ekaterina thought it was something
more substantial.

Early in August 1911 the Cheberyak children became sick,
and this at a time when Vera and the children had been
constantly questioned by the authorities. The illness got worse
and the children were taken to the hospital. Their mother was
in custody, and upon being released, rushed straight to the
hospital and took Zhenya home in defiance of the hospital
personnel who warned her that his condition was grave.
Within two days Zhenya died. The turn of events seemed
highly suspicious, and I instructed my aides Vygranov and
Polishchuk to keep a close eye on the Cheberyaks. I thought
that Zhenya, who was often delirious, might reveal something.
Intermittently, Zhenya was unconscious, and during the brief
periods when he regained consciousness, his mother kept
warning him, "Tell them that I had nothing to do with it," and
the boy whispered in agony, "Mama, leave me alone" or cried
out, "Andrey, don't scream—don't scream!"

PRESIDING JUDGE: You heard these words yourself, or you were
told about them?

WITNESS: It was reported to me by my agents, who never left
the premises.

PRESIDING JUDGE: Were you there too from time to time?

WITNESS: Of course. I dropped in often for ten minutes or so to
see if my agents were doing their job. When Zhenya cried out
those words, his mother leaned over and smothered his words
with kisses. Soon thereafter, he died. Cheberyak's other
daughter, Valya, was also gravely ill and I gathered, from the
Dyakonov sisters, that Vera Cheberyak paid hardly any attention to her daughter's illness. A woman doctor of Vera's acquaintance dropped in occasionally to check on Valya's condition and prescribed medication, but the prescriptions were
never filled. She used to lock the children in their rooms and

left them for the whole day, while she was socializing with her friend Adele Ravich. Thus, Valya too passed away eleven days following Zhenya's demise.

PRESIDING JUDGE: This information you obtained as a private investigator?

WITNESS: Yes indeed. Including the information about Vera Cheberyak's criminal contacts. She entertained thieves and robbers, who came dressed in uniforms of government officials or university students and walked out wearing shabby overalls. It was clear to me that her home served as a meeting place for crooks where plans were hatched—whom and where to rob.

I passed the information on to Brazul, telling him that I could use some assistance in keeping track of the activities of these characters. Brazul said that he was in touch with a student who would be willing to help. This is how I met Machalin, who seemed intelligent and bright to render valuable service. I briefed him about Cheberyak and her associates, telling him that I was especially interested in Vera's brother, Singayevsky, who I was convinced was involved in Yushchinsky's murder.

Machalin brought up the name of Karayev, a convicted anarchist, whose daring exploits as a revolutionary made him well known and highly admired in the underworld. Karayev was due to arrive in Kiev in a few days, and Machalin arranged to bring us together. After some hesitation, Karayev agreed to cooperate. Our plan was to involve Singayevsky in an attempt to gain the release of a known robber named Fatisov, a relative of Singayevsky's who was convicted for armed robbery and was to be transferred from the Kiev lockup to a more secure prison facility elsewhere. We thought in this manner to gain Singayevsky's confidence and ascertain his involvement in the Yushchinsky case.

Subsequently, Karayev met Singayevsky several times and in the course of the last meeting he told Singayevsky that he, Karayev, was summoned to police headquarters and overheard several police officials intimating that they were about to arrest Singayevsky, Latyshev, and Rudzinsky. Singayevsky became extremely agitated, explaining that this was the work of the "bitches" Dyakonov, who would pay dearly for their "big mouths." He said that he and his friends would break into police headquarters that same night, steal the data pertaining to their case, and if need be, "waste" Colonel Ivanove, who was in charge of the investigation. He continued to ramble on, saying that it was the "minister's brain" of Rudzinsky that was responsible for the bungled job. Karayev's conversations with Singayevsky were witnessed by Machalin who was to be involved in "springing" Fatisov.

In the course of my official investigation of the Yushchinsky murder, I identified the following items of clothing found on or around the corpse: a jacket, a shirt, a cap, and a strip of a pillowcase. In questioning the Dyakonov sisters, I learned that Vera Cheberyak had asked them to make her several pillow-cases, which they did. According to the Dyakonov sisters, the embroidery on the pillowcases was identical with the embroi-dered pattern on the piece of material found on the body. I informed Brazul about the pillowcase, who in turn communi-cated the information to the police authorities; several days thereafter, the newspapers carried stories about the alleged new evidence.

When the story about the pillowcase appeared in print, Brazul received a letter from one Shwechko, a barber, in-forming him that he, the barber, was privy to important infor-mation about the case. I paid a visit to Shwechko's barbershop and questioned him. He told me that when he saw the photos of the alleged perpetrators of the crime—namely Latyshev, Singayevsky, Rudzinsky, and Vera Cheberyak—he recalled having been under arrest in the same cell with Rudzinsky. At night, he overheard a whispered conversation between Rud-zinsky and another prisoner alongside of him. The prisoner asked, "Why did you have to kill the boy?" and Rudzinsky answered, "Because he squealed."

PRESIDING JUDGE: Shwechko told you that?

WITNESS: Yes.

PRESIDING JUDGE: Is he too a habitual criminal?

WITNESS: Shwechko owned a barbershop frequented by all types of shady characters. Over the barbershop he kept several rooms for the convenience of out-of-town and local criminals. I gathered from Shwechko that Rudzinsky and his friends planned a major break-in into the Sophist Cathedral, which was surrounded by a high fence, making entry well-nigh impossible, especially for a grown-up person. Thus the boy Yushchinsky was inveigled to join them in order to facilitate the job. He was supposed to squeeze through the grated fence and open the gate from the inside. This was Shwechko's story. Soon thereafter, I was charged with forgery while in service and was arrested and imprisoned. I spent a month and a half in jail but was subsequently acquitted. Hence I took no further part in the investigation.

PRESIDING JUDGE: With regard to Krasovsky's assertion that he deems it relevant to disclose intimate details of Vera Cheberyak's relations with her husband—if this is hearsay, the court is not interested in listening to rumors.

WITNESS: I heard it from Vera herself.

PRESIDING JUDGE: She told it to you personally?

WITNESS: Yes, she did.

PRESIDING JUDGE: Do the sides consider the information relevant to the case before us?

PROSECUTOR: In view of the fact that Vera Cheberyak has not been implicated as a defendant, having appeared before us as a witness, details of her married life are of no interest to me.

ZAMISLOVSKI: We share the prosecutor's view, but if the defense will insist on having this disclosed in open court, we shall not object.

KARABCHEVSKY: The defense is also not interested in this information.

PRESIDING JUDGE: Since Vera Cheberyak is not a defendant in the case, and both sides having expressed total disinterest in this information, it is the ruling of this court that information pertaining to the intimate life of the Cheberyaks is irrelevant to this case and shall not be part of the court record.

Interrogation of Krasovsky

PROSECUTOR: I understand that you had a successful career in the police department. Tell me about it in a few words. You have apparently attracted the attention of the authorities. Did you participate in solving a major murder case?

WITNESS: Yes, I did.

PROSECUTOR: So your fame as a detective is attributable to that case?

WITNESS: Yes.

PROSECUTOR: When you began your recent assignment, did you familiarize yourself with the Zaitsev estate?

WITNESS: Yes.

PROSECUTOR: Did you examine the fence separating the Marra estate from the Zaitsev estate?

WITNESS: Yes I did—thoroughly.

PROSECUTOR: Did you find it in good repair? Were there any holes in the fence?

WITNESS: There were a number of openings in the fence.

PROSECUTOR: In the event that it was necessary to carry out a body, say at night, from one estate to the other, was that possible?

WITNESS: Certainly it was possible.

PROSECUTOR: Obviously you looked over the Zaitsev estate. Did you make a list of the people working there? The Jews staying there?

WITNESS: Certainly. I have a full list of all those who lived on the premises.

PROSECUTOR: Did you know Beilis, chat with him?

WITNESS: Yes, I did.

PROSECUTOR: Did you know him?

WITNESS: No. I didn't.

PROSECUTOR: I cannot understand, in view of your experience as a detective, on what basis you suspected and detained for days and weeks some of Yushchinsky's relatives who subsequently proved to be totally innocent of the crime.

WITNESS: It was reported to me that Andrey's stepfather, Luka Prihodko, mistreated the boy; there were also some deaths in the family under mysterious circumstances.

PROSECUTOR: Is this again some of your hearsay evidence? Where was the information coming from?

WITNESS: I learned that from their neighbors.

PROSECUTOR: Name some of these neighbors.

WITNESS: I can't recall now—it was a long time ago.

PROSECUTOR: Did you investigate the possibility that Jews including Beilis may have been involved in the crime? The record indicates that in July you admitted the possibility that the murder was committed by Jews for ritual purposes.

WITNESS: I consulted the magistrate every step of the way. We explored all kinds of possibilities including the version you just brought up.

PROSECUTOR: Is there any official record to the effect that the murder was committed on the Zaitsev estate and that Beilis may have been involved?

WITNESS: There may have been such a record, however, this assumption was laid to rest in the course of my investigation.

PROSECUTOR: When Beilis was arrested didn't you complain to Brazul that "it's completely incomprehensible to me why an innocent man is being blamed for the crime"?

WITNESS: Yes, there was such an occasion.

PROSECUTOR: Yes indeed. You were outraged when Beilis was arrested, weren't you?

WITNESS: Yes, I was puzzled.

PROSECUTOR: Tell me, Beilis was arrested on the third of March. Was Vera Cheberyak arrested about the same time?

WITNESS: As I recall, the police search was made at both places simultaneously.

PROSECUTOR: When Vera Cheberyak was detained and Beilis was arrested, didn't you appear at the Cheberyak flat and try to gain the children's confidence, bringing them candy and pastries?

WITNESS: Yes, I did.

PROSECUTOR: Who did you come with?

WITNESS: With Vygranov and Polishchuk.

PROSECUTOR: Do you recall where you bought the pastries?

WITNESS: I don't remember. The children were frightened and in a nontalkative mood. I tried gently to draw them out. Therefore, I had to resort to bringing them candy and cakes, but such petty details as to where it was bought I did not record.

PROSECUTOR: There were some rumors that Yushchinsky knew some Jews in Slabodka. Were you familiar with those rumors?

WITNESS: There were such rumors.

PROSECUTOR: When did the fairy tale about the switches arise—that Yushchinsky, Zhenya, and one other boy cut off some switches and Andrey's switch looked better than Zhenya's and that they quarreled and one threatened to tell Yushchinsky's aunt and another threatened to squeal to the police? When did that story originate?

WITNESS: These reports reached me in July. I heard it from the janitor at the public drinking faucet.

PROSECUTOR: Did you manage to find the third boy who apparently witnessed this discussion?

WITNESS: We didn't look for him.

PROSECUTOR: Was there an assumption following the alleged quarrel that Vera Cheberyak, with the help of the underworld, decided to kill Yushchinsky and that an hour later Yushchinsky appeared? Tell me, what was the implication of this fairy tale? There was a quarrel, a falling out, one threatened the other. What was the connection to Cheberyak?

WITNESS: Zhenya rushed home and told about the quarrel and the threats. Two other persons were present when Zhenya told his story. Thereafter they remarked that Yushchinsky ought to be "calmed down." He shouldn't tattle. Finally the two characters said should it become necessary he ought to be "taken care of."

PROSECUTOR: Who told you about this conversation—about "calming down" and "taken care of?"

WITNESS: I heard this from Mrs. Lepetsky.

PROSECUTOR: Oh—Mrs. Lepetsky! Tell me please, did the evidence assembled by you constantly point in the direction of Cheberyak? What evidence did you have concerning Cheberyak? The fact that she maintained a den frequented by suspicious characters, or did you have something more definite?

WITNESS: My investigation continually led me to Cheberyak. For instance, the theory about ritual murders originated with her. She talked about it, she spread rumors about it, she distributed flyers stressing the same thing.

PROSECUTOR: Did she distribute the flyers? Surely more than one person distributed flyers.

WITNESS: It was reported that she brought her flyers to the office of the prosecution, handed them out to anyone she came across.

PROSECUTOR: How did you perceive Cheberyak's connection to the Yushchinsky murder? You had a notion that she was involved in the crime in order to precipitate a pogrom?

WITNESS: Yes, she was a participant in the murder.

PROSECUTOR: In order to set the stage for a pogrom?

WITNESS: The aim was one. To get rid of a dangerous witness, who was in cahoots with a gang, who knew a great deal about the gang's present and past activities. The rumors about the murder having been committed by Jews stemmed from her, and I saw in this a maneuver to mislead the authorities.

PROSECUTOR: In other words, there were two aims—one, to get rid of the boy who knew the gang's secrets and, two, to stimulate a pogrom inasmuch as she handed out the flyers.

WITNESS: Yes.

PROSECUTOR: You said that rumors abounded to the effect that she was in possession of large quantities of stolen goods gained from previous pogroms, and that she accumulated so much silk that she used it as fuel for her stove—to bake cakes with. Where did this fairy tale originate?

WITNESS: This I heard from the Dyakonov sisters.

PROSECUTOR: You actually believed the story that she used silk to bake cakes?

WITNESS: Yes. Because she traded with stolen goods—sold it cheaply. She had on hand silver as well as silk, but the disposal of these goods was forced upon her by frequent searches in her flat by the police. I presume that this prompted her to burn the silk.

PROSECUTOR: Tell me please, did you establish the fact that Cheberyak knew Beilis? Did you ascertain other particulars indicating that apart from the criminal world she was also acquainted with Beilis?

WITNESS: I had a record of all her acquaintances, but I had no special reason to dwell on her acquaintanceship with Beilis.

PROSECUTOR: Didn't you tell the magistrate that you had reason to believe that the relationship between Cheberyak and Beilis was rather close?

WITNESS: I was denied the right to explain it fully. When I wanted to touch upon it, the court found it inadmissible.

PROSECUTOR: How do you explain that from one aspect Cheberyak was so well-off that she didn't deny herself the luxury of using silk as fuel, yet during your search you found her pillow bare, without a pillowcase?

WITNESS: She wasn't well-off. Only on rare occasions did she have on hand expensive stuff; however, members of the gang behaved as if there was no tomorrow—drinking, carousing, going to the races, and wearing nice clothes. They spent money freely and recklessly.

PROSECUTOR: Tell me please, you reentered the case in early February. Didn't you write to Brazul offering your services as an investigator, or did he invite your help?

WITNESS: I never wrote such a letter.

PROSECUTOR: You apparently spent a great deal of money treating the Dyakonov sisters to drinks and meals in various restaurants. Did that come out of your own pocket?

WITNESS: Yes, out of my own pocket.

PROSECUTOR: Did the Dyakonov women really impress you as credible witnesses?

WITNESS: Yes. When they gave me information I always tried to verify it from other sources, but I did attach a great deal of importance to what they were saying.

PROSECUTOR: Please respond to the following question, but briefly and distinctly, as I find detailed answers most wearisome. Did the Dyakonov sisters ever tell you that Rudzinsky and Singayevsky killed Yushchinsky and that Vera (Cheberyak) related this fact to the Dyakonov sisters "out of friendship?"

WITNESS: Yes, they did.

PROSECUTOR: Thus, the Dyakonov women first learned of the murder from Vera?

WITNESS: I cannot say precisely whether they did or not.

PROSECUTOR: Now for the last question: are you aware that Karayev once served in the secret police?

WITNESS: He did not.

PROSECUTOR: One question about Shwechko. You knew that Shwechko was in prison. That he had overheard a conversation between Rudzinsky and another person and that he recalled the conversation when Rudzinsky appeared. He heard the following words: "On account of this kid, etc., etc. it was necessary to get rid of him. He shouldn't snitch, etc." What does Shwechko do? Is he a barber?

WITNESS: Yes.

PROSECUTOR: Did this same Shwechko let you in on the details: the boy Yushchinsky knew all the gang's secrets, that he was to be used in the robbery? Did Shwechko tell you all that?

WITNESS: Yes, among other things.

PROSECUTOR: Among other things? That the boy will collaborate in robbing the Sophist Cathedral. Surely you knew that Yushchinsky was a religious boy—that he wanted to become a priest. Did you know that when you heard those details?

WITNESS: Yes, I did.

PROSECUTOR: Still you believed it?

WITNESS: Absolutely. The prosecutor's question calls for an explanation.

PRESIDING JUDGE: Please explain.

WITNESS: From the information available to me, Yushchinsky was a secretive boy and not as virtuous as he was portrayed here.

PRESIDING JUDGE: Did you know him personally?

WITNESS: No, I did not.

ZAMISLOVSKI: You said you were convinced that Andrey was deficient?

WITNESS: Yes.

ZAMISLOVSKI: The boy who fasted, went to confession—you consider him capable of being an accessory to a robbery?

WITNESS: Yes, I did.

ZAMISLOVSKI: You also testified that Alexandra and Luka Prihodko treated him cruelly; how did you establish that? Through whom?

WITNESS: This was confirmed by Nezhinsky and partly by

Natalia Yushchinsky; the boy spent more time with his aunt than with his mother.

ZAMISLOVSKI: Is that what the Prihodkos testified to before the magistrate?

WITNESS: I wasn't present during their testimony.

ZAMISLOVSKI: Thus what they told the investigator, you don't know, yet you consider that an established fact.

WITNESS: This was also confirmed by Vera Cheberyak.

ZAMISLOVSKI: But surely you didn't attach any credence to Cheberyak? According to your story, which you attributed to Natalia Yushchinsky, the boy used to spend a great deal of time at the Cheberyak home and lying about it, claiming he was at school.

WITNESS: Yes.

ZAMISLOVSKI: Did you relay this to the magistrate, or is this a brand-new revelation?

WITNESS: I can't recall precisely whether I reported it to the magistrate or not. Most likely I did.

ZAMISLOVSKI: It was you who suspected Prihodko and had him arrested. How long was he in detention?

WITNESS: I can't recall.

ZAMISLOVSKI: Approximately.

WITNESS: Perhaps several days.

ZAMISLOVSKI: Ten to twenty days? You were so precise in your testimony, yet now you are experiencing lapses of memory.

WITNESS: I can't remember every minor detail.

ZAMISLOVSKI: We don't know yet whether this was a minor detail. You also had him shaved and his hair cut to facilitate identification, did you not?

WITNESS: I did because the sources I relied on at the time suggested that the suspect was clean shaven but at the time of his arrest he had a beard.

ZAMISLOVSKI: You seem to have carried on your investigation in all directions.

WITNESS: When the suspects came up with incontrovertible alibis, they were released.

ZAMISLOVSKI: Now a few questions about Karayev and Machalin. You said that Karayev was in prison for possessing explosives and you knew that when he identified himself as an anarchist communist.

WITNESS: Yes, I knew.

ZAMISLOVSKI: So what transpired was that you, a former commander of the secret police, worked hand in hand with a former anarchist communist. Is that it?

WITNESS: At that time he lived in Kiev, as you well know, and that fact was known to those concerned with supervising the anarchist party. To the best of my recollection, when I got acquainted with him he did not belong to any party and I felt no embarrassment meeting him and utilizing his services.

ZAMISLOVSKI: Hence, working with a known anarchist communist did not embarrass you and you found nothing wrong collaborating with a man who was in prison for the possession of bombs. How about him? Didn't it bother him, working with an officer of the secret police?

WITNESS: He didn't know who he was dealing with. He knew me as Ivan Karasev.

ZAMISLOVSKI: He never found out?

WITNESS: He did, but only after we had utilized his services.

ZAMISLOVSKI: Utilized his services—what do you mean by that phrase?

WITNESS: In this context it meant that he had fulfilled the task he was asked to perform: he had seen Singayevsky, he succeeded in gaining his confidence and tricked him into confessing.

ZAMISLOVSKI: Didn't it occur to you why a former anarchist communist had chosen to get involved in this case?

WITNESS: My concern was to obtain information. His political creed and private life were of no interest to me.

ZAMISLOVSKI: Possessing bombs you call private affairs?

WITNESS: Certainly. He may believe in certain causes which I don't share; to sort out his beliefs was not my concern.

ZAMISLOVSKI: That wasn't my question. I asked you what moved a man, a known anarchist communist, to stick his nose in this investigation?

WITNESS: I presume he was stirred by such a senseless inexplicable crime.

ZAMISLOVSKI: When did he arrive in Kiev?

WITNESS: I don't know precisely. His movements did not interest me.

ZAMISLOVSKI: That's amazing. You seem to know everything so well, but when we reach a certain point, you suddenly don't remember. I ask you, when did he arrive in Kiev?

WITNESS: I don't know. I didn't know it then, and I don't know it now.

ZAMISLOVSKI: How did you get acquainted with Karayev?

WITNESS: Through Machalin.

ZAMISLOVSKI: You met him at a hotel?

WITNESS: Yes.

ZAMISLOVSKI: What was the gist of your conversation?

WITNESS: I can't recall the details, but I made a proposal to him. I told him that he had ties to the underworld, there having been an incident in prison which earned him a great deal of respect and admiration on the part of the prisoners; he thus gained influence and the confidence of the criminal elements.

ZAMISLOVSKI: The picture I surmise is as follows: a total stranger approaches an anarchist communist and propositions him. "You are familiar with the criminal world." And then what?

WITNESS: Machalin was present, and he knew Karayev for some time.

ZAMISLOVSKI: What was his response?

WITNESS: He said he would let me know in a day or two.

ZAMISLOVSKI: What did Singayevsky tell you about his confession, since you seem to remember every detail. How did he express himself?

WITNESS: I already reported that.

ZAMISLOVSKI: No, you did not. You made some references to Rudzinsky, but that is not sufficient. Where did the confession take place?

WITNESS: In the hotel.

ZAMISLOVSKI: Did Karayev and Machalin report to you that they got Singayevsky drunk?

WITNESS: Yes.

ZAMISLOVSKI: How? With vodka?

WITNESS: That's the usual method.

ZAMISLOVSKI: This may well be the usual method, but for an anarchist communist and his student accomplice, this was not a usual method.

WITNESS: We're not talking about an anarchist and a student. We had in mind the criminal.

ZAMISLOVSKI: Well, once he was drunk, what did he say? Didn't he say that they all left for Moscow the same day?

WITNESS: Yes, he did.

ZAMISLOVSKI: The same day?

WITNESS: The same day.

ZAMISLOVSKI: Now you remember this little detail, but previously it was erased from your memory.

WITNESS: You reminded me.

ZAMISLOVSKI: And didn't Karayev and Machalin tell you that Karayev did not play out his role, that he frightened Singayevsky and the latter did not tell you anything of substance?

WITNESS: Yes, I was apprehensive about Karayev becoming overenthusiastic about his assignment and at a crucial point he might fail the test. He may have tipped him off with an indiscreet word and made him suspicious.

SHMAKOV: There were two periods in your investigative activities in this case—until September 8, 1911, at which time you were relieved from your assignment, and then again beginning with April 1912.

WITNESS: Yes.

SHMAKOV: The data that you collected during the second period convinced you that this case was the result of a gang of thieves—not a ritual murder—is that right?

WITNESS: Yes.

SHMAKOV: Was this your opinion throughout your investigation?

WITNESS: Yes.

SHMAKOV: Did you know Pincus—Beilis's boy?

WITNESS: Yes.

SHMAKOV: Was Pincus acquainted with Zhenya and Andrey—were they all friends?

WITNESS: There was nothing to indicate that they were close friends.

SHMAKOV: You testified that Pincus, Andrey, and Zhenya Cheberyak were friends.

WITNESS: It wasn't precisely so. They knew each other, played together, but there was no friendship.

SHMAKOV: You didn't deny that it was so reported by you, yet when you asked Pincus whether he knew Andrey and Zhenya what was his reply?

WITNESS: He answered that he didn't know them. For me his reply was understandable.

SHMAKOV: Yet your conclusion was that he lied.

WITNESS: Yes, he lied.

SHMAKOV: Didn't you tell the magistrate that the kiln was the most likely site for the murder?

WITNESS: If one believed in the possibility that the crime was ritualistic and that Beilis was involved, then that would have been the most convenient place.

SHMAKOV: But your statement mentioned neither Beilis nor the ritualistic aspects, it said that if a murder was committed, then it was in the kiln. When you viewed the articles found on the body of the murdered boy, did you find traces of clay on them?

WITNESS: Yes, I already testified to that.

SHMAKOV: Didn't you then come to the conclusion that the murder was committed within the area of the brick factory?

WITNESS: No, I didn't, because such an assumption would have been promptly refuted.

SHMAKOV: I am asking you whether your testimony before the magistrate included the assumption that the murder was committed within the area of the Zaitsev factory because there was clay on the site while everywhere else there was snow.

WITNESS: Yes, there was such an assumption.

SHMAKOV: Then you said that the murder was an act of vengeance and consequently there were a series of searches at Vera Cheberyak's flat?

WITNESS: Yes, various circumstances strengthened the conviction that the murder was an act of vengeance.

SHMAKOV: How did you report your conviction? The body was lying around at Vera Cheberyak's flat on the twelfth, the thirteenth, and the fourteenth of March. Surely she was fearful of a new search, yet you confirm that she had the body for three days.

WITNESS: On the basis of the information then available to me, the body was at the Cheberyak flat in the small room for three consecutive days.

SHMAKOV: How do you reconcile the two facts—Cheberyak's fear of a search and holding the body in her flat?

WITNESS: She was in a state of helplessness, she was abandoned by her collaborators, some of whom left for Moscow and the others in jail. She was flustered that she could not carry out the body.

PRESIDING JUDGE: You said that she was always surrounded by a strange "assortment of friends"; if some of them were under arrest, it didn't necessarily follow that she was devoid of assistance.

WITNESS: The criminal world adheres to a well-known rite, that once a certain place is targeted for frequent searches, which in their jargon was called "the berry was crushed," criminals avoided it as a pest.

SHMAKOV:How do you explain the facts that Cheberyak not only held the body in her flat but leaving her home left the corpse "unguarded?"

WITNESS: Yes, she had been going out to see the Dyakonov sisters.

SHMAKOV: Hence no one stayed behind. How do you explain that?

WITNESS: She was totally confused.

SHMAKOV: You incurred considerable expenses in connection with your investigation, didn't you?

WITNESS: Yes.

SHMAKOV: And you covered all those expenses yourself? For what purpose?

WITNESS: I was involved in this case as a matter of principle. To ascertain all the circumstances surrounding the crime, it was for me a matter of high priority, since my activities had been judged as incorrect.

GRUZENBERG: You testified that on the morning of March 22, Dr. Karpinsky told a member of the Kiev city council, Burchak: "I have not yet performed the autopsy but received a letter describing the stab wounds." Is that what you testified to?

WITNESS: That's correct.

PRESIDING JUDGE: Was the conversation in your presence, or someone told you about it?

WITNESS: It was reported to me that Karpinsky handed the letter to Burchak.

GRUZENBERG: And the letter referred to stab wounds and that the murder was committed by Jews?

WITNESS: Yes.

PRESIDING JUDGE: Who told you about it?

WITNESS: I can't recall, but I feel sure that Burchak and Karpinsky would confirm it.

ZAMISLOVSKI: This is hearsay evidence.

PRESIDING JUDGE: It appears that you don't know who reported that to you.

WITNESS: At present I don't recall, but definite persons were referred to.

ZAMISLOVSKI: Let the record show that he doesn't know the source of this information.

GRUZENBERG: I will now proceed with my interrogation. These persons mentioned by Karayev as having taken part in the murder, they left for Moscow. When?

WITNESS: The following day.

GRUZENBERG: What was the date?

WITNESS: On the thirteenth.

GRUZENBERG: But you were told they left the same day.

WITNESS: Yes, Machalin said they left the same day.

GRUZENBERG: But in fact they traveled the following day.

WITNESS: Yes.

GRUZENBERG: Was it established that on the day of the murder a robbery took place? And if so, where?

WITNESS: In the optical store of Adamovich, goods valued at 2500 rubles were taken.

GRUZENBERG: What kind of goods?

WITNESS: Optical instruments, binoculars, knives.

GRUZENBERG: Are you aware that in the aftermath of the robbery, when the murder was attributed to Vera Cheberyak and her cohorts, one of them admitted having taken part in the robbery?

WITNESS: Yes.

GRUZENBERG: Why did he volunteer this information?

WITNESS: In this way they had hoped to clear themselves, that is, to prove that since they were involved in the robbery, they couldn't have committed the murder.

GRUZENBERG: Yet the murder was committed in the morning, while the robbery took place at night?

WITNESS: Yes indeed.

GRUZENBERG: How did they expect to clear themselves? If they participated in the robbery at night, this does not preclude their involvement in the murder in the morning. How did they explain that?

WITNESS: They apparently overlooked the fact that their cover was invalid.

GRUZENBERG: Are you familiar with the fact that, in spite of their confession, they were not prosecuted?

WITNESS: Yes. The case was scheduled and subsequently terminated.

GRUZENBERG: A man comes forward and admits having committed a crime, yet no judicial proceedings followed?

WITNESS: Yes.

GRUZENBERG: Now what was Ekaterina Dyakonov's explanation with regard to the pillowcases?

WITNESS: She sewed it for Cheberyak.

GRUZENBERG: Vera Cheberyak gave her a pattern to follow?

WITNESS: Yes, she gave Dyakonov an old pillowcase as a sample.

GRUZENBERG: Was there a similarity between that sample and the strip of pillowcase found on the murdered boy?

WITNESS: A remarkable similarity.

GRUZENBERG: You testified before magistrate Mashkevitz for three consecutive days? On which dates?

WITNESS: On the thirteenth, fourteenth, and fifteenth of July. On the sixteenth, I was home, and on the seventeenth I was arrested and sent to jail.

GRUZENBERG: What were you accused of? Was it in connection with this case?

WITNESS: I was accused of taking a bribe in a previous case.

GRUZENBERG: You were held in jail for a month and a half. Who tried you?

WITNESS: The Kiev district court.

GRUZENBERG: You were acquitted and exonerated?

WITNESS: Yes.

GRUZENBERG: Thus you were denied your freedom needlessly, kept in prison on a charge of bribery, and then acquitted?

PRESIDING JUDGE TO GRUZENBERG: You have no right to judge the actions of the government prosecutor. When a prisoner is accused and then acquitted, it doesn't necessarily mean that he was denied his freedom needlessly.

GRUZENBERG: Let me rephrase my question. What it amounts to is that you were kept in jail for a month and a half in a case in which you were acquitted?

WITNESS: Yes.

KARABCHEVSKY: Has it been established that Andrey Yushchinsky left home on the morning of March twelfth wearing a coat, and was then seen with Zhenya Cheberyak, but without a coat?

WITNESS: Yes.

KARABCHEVSKY: Thereafter, no one has seen him?

WITNESS: This was established.

KARABCHEVSKY: Thus, no matter which version one accepts about the murder, one thing is certain. The last time anyone has seen Yushchinsky alive, he was without a coat?

WITNESS: Yes.

KARABCHEVSKY: What happened to the coat? Where do you think it disappeared to?

WITNESS: In spite of my strenuous efforts to ascertain the location of the coat, I haven't been successful.

KARABCHEVSKY: Now about your incarceration on an illegal charge of bribery. When was that supposed to have occurred?

WITNESS: In 1903.

KARABCHEVSKY: How do you explain the long delay in bringing you to justice? Was the alleged crime uncovered only recently?

WITNESS: The usual procedure among officials in the event of an impropriety or crime having been committed by a government employee is for the official involved to be summoned for an explanation. No one asked me for an explanation, the charge and the imprisonment having been initiated simultaneously.

KARABCHEVSKY: When you were drilled by magistrate Mashkevitz for three consecutive days, did you know then that the charge of bribery allegedly committed in 1903 was pending against you?

WITNESS: No, I didn't, although members of the Double-Headed Eagle spread the word around that Krasovsky was facing imprisonment. I paid no attention to those rumors, but apparently they were better informed as to what's pending than I.

KARABCHEVSKY: The civil prosecutor questioned you about your contacts with a known bomber, anarchist, etc. Was this anarchist tried and served his time in prison?

WITNESS: Yes.

KARABCHEVSKY: When you contacted him, did you know that he was a dangerous anarchist and bomber?

WITNESS: No, I had no reason to suspect that, as I have had no dealings with him.

KARABCHEVSKY: As far as you were concerned, he was tried, deported, yet the authorities knew that he was in Kiev?

WITNESS: Yes.

KARABCHEVSKY: And in the course of your conversation with him, he had no bombs, nor did he preach anarchy—or did he?

WITNESS: I've had no political discussions with him.

GRUZENBERG: Are you familiar with a certain Pavlovich?

WITNESS: Yes.

GRUZENBERG: What connection does he have to Cheberyak?

WITNESS: He is a member of the Double-Headed Eagle and appears in police records as a thief and a robber. He served time in 1908 upon conviction by the Kiev circuit court.

GRUZENBERG: What was his crime?

WITNESS: Embezzlement and breaking and entering. In 1910 he was again arrested on suspicion of robbery.

GRUZENBERG: Is it known to you that Pavlovich had been distributing leaflets at Yushchinsky's funeral?

WITNESS: Yes, he was arrested passing out leaflets.

GRUZENBERG: The same convicted thief and robber was arrested for distributing leaflets?

WITNESS: Yes.

PRESIDING JUDGE: Since you hadn't been at the funeral, where did you get your information?

WITNESS: This was well known in police circles.

GRUZENBERG: Was he subjected to any administrative action by the governor or his representative?

WITNESS: This I don't recall. I know that he was arrested along with another member of the Double-Headed Eagle, Pashchenko, on suspicion of swindling 500 rubles from the postal authorities.

PRESIDING JUDGE: Didn't you tell Golubev that the murder was committed for ritual purposes?

WITNESS: Not in such categorical form, but conversations referring to that possibility did take place. I realized that Golubev and others belonging to monarchist organizations zealously clung to the theory of this being a ritual murder, and when contradicted, they raised an awful clamor. This was widely reported in the newspapers. To avoid needless arguments, I usually told these people, "Yes, that's a possibility." I was under no obligation to share my findings with them; my responsibility was to report only to the governor.

PRESIDING JUDGE: You did not report to the magistrate that the murder was ritually motivated?

WITNESS: No.

PRESIDING JUDGE: Do I understand you to say that you agreed with Golubev only in order to appease him?

WITNESS: I reluctantly agreed with the version he tried to foist on me.

WITNESS (addressing judge): Your honor, I have just learned that the police came to my home in my absence and started an inquest . . .

PRESIDING JUDGE: This does not concern this court. You should apply to the governor.

WITNESS: Police are questioning members of my family . . . I am extremely agitated and cannot remain here. Your honor, I beg to be released.

PRESIDING JUDGE: In view of this exceptional circumstance, do the sides agree to release this witness?

PROSECUTOR: Certainly.

KARABCHEVSKY: I petition the court to enter into the record in what anguished state the witness was forced to leave the witness stand. We consider it germane to his testimony.

PRESIDING JUDGE: This is a personal matter. What relation does it have to his testimony?

БЕЙЛИСЪ.

Mendel Beilis, the accused.

Feodor A. Boldyrev, presiding judge at the Beilis trial.

Members of the Prosecution and Defense Teams

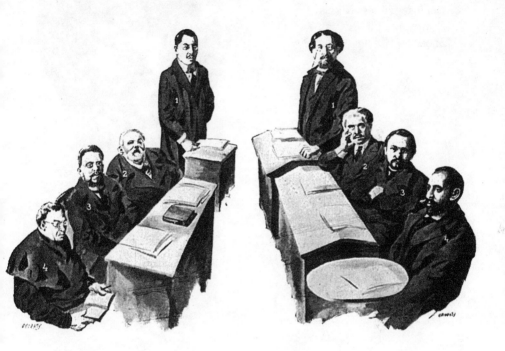

Prosecution	Defense
1. O. V. Vipper	1. Oscar Gruzenberg
2. S. Shmakov	2. N. B. Karabchevsky
3. G. G. Zamislovski	3. V. A. Maklakov
4. Religious expert	4. A. S. Zarudny
Father Justin Pranaitis	

Defense witness Nikolai Krasovsky, the Russian Sherlock Holmes.

Defense witness Brazul-Brushkovsky, journalist.

Professor Kosorotov, medical expert for the prosecution.

Chaplinsky, state prosecutor and conspirator against Beilis.

The Real Murderers?

Vera Cheberyak

Piotr Singayevsky

Boris Rudzinsky

Ivan Latyshev

Mendel Beilis with his family after the trial.

אין אָנדיינקונג פון בײלים פּראָצעס.

„צאָר ניקאָלאַי"
צו מענדעל בײלים:

„גיי מענדעל. ביזם פריי!
פרעה זיך מיט דײנע אַמעריקאַ-
נער פריינדע, אָבער איך וועל
זיך שוין אָפרעכענען פיר דיין
בעפראַיונג, מיט דיינע איבער-
געבליבענע רוסישע בריודער."

בײלים ניט שולדיג – די יודען יאָ שולדיג.

Drawing of Czar Nicholas telling Beilis, "Go celebrate
with your American friends, but I'll square accounts
with your fellow Russian Jews."

6

The Young Revolutionary

A young revolutionary who had several brushes with the law in connection with his antigovernment activities, Sergei Machalin, as a young boy, had witnessed a pogrom, the horror of which had affected the course of his life.

He had been a student at an agricultural school, worked on the railroad, gave private lessons to disadvantaged youth, and dreamed of a career in opera. In 1911, he came into a small legacy from his grandfather, which enabled him to devote more time to revolutionary activities. Press reports on the Beilis case struck him as another conspiracy invented by the czarist government; but what impelled him to get involved in the Yushchinsky murder was the pervasive anti-Semitic agitation fueled by the notorious Union of the Russian People and its local surrogate, the Double-Headed Eagle, a campaign which threatened to explode into a full-scale pogrom. Having met Brazul-Brushkovsky before, Machalin decided to seek him out and offer his services. Brazul had serious reservations about enlisting the services of a known "leftist"—with an agenda of his own—but Machalin insisted, intimating that he had an "ace up his sleeve."

The ace turned out to be Amzor Karayev, a young revolutionary of Machalin's age, but one with much more impressive, indeed extraordinary, credentials. In his testimony before the investigating magistrate a year before the trial, Karayev described himself as a "nobleman" and a native of the Caucasus. However, his police record revealed him to be a rebel against the existing order with a long record of imprisonment for political activities.

While in prison, Karayev acquired a legendary reputation within the underworld as a fearless, reckless rebel who "never bowed to authority."

It was a man with Karayev's background, Machalin argued, that could uncover the identity of the criminal elements linked to the Yushchinsky case. In his testimony at the trial, Machalin revealed how he had summoned Karayev to come to Kiev from the Caucasus on a matter of "serious import." Karayev understood the invitation from Machalin to be connected with internal party matters and it required all the persuasive powers Machalin could muster to get the impulsive Karayev to agree to cooperate in an investigation unrelated to revolutionary activity. What finally persuaded Karayev to get involved was Machalin's argument that by participating in an investigation designed to expose the government's cabal in the Yushchinsky case, Karayev might regain his credibility within the "party," some of whose members had accused him of being an agent provocateur.

Machalin arranged for Brazul and Krasovsky to meet Karayev at a hotel room in Kiev in order to decide on a course of action. (Krasovsky used an assumed name in his first contact with Karayev. Disclosing that he had previously served as chief of the Kiev secret police would have discredited him in the eyes of the young revolutionary.) Krasovsky expressed his conviction that Rudzinsky, Latyshev, and Singayevsky were the perpetrators of the Yushchinsky murder, but that the key to the solution of the crime was Vera Cheberyak. Of the three criminals referred to by Krasovsky, Laty-

shev was dead, having jumped to his death from a window in the
Kiev lockup, Rudzinsky was serving time in Siberia for armed
robbery, leaving only Singayevsky on the loose. With Cheberyak
being under constant police surveillance, Karayev decided to "work
over" the dull-witted Singayevsky. Singayevsky was awestruck
when an intermediary introduced him to the legendary Karayev.
The latter was prepared with a suitable scenario: he had a job in
mind that required people with "steady hands." Singayevsky was
impressed. He was prepared for a "wet" job ("wet" meaning a job
that entailed killing), and he could secure competent accomplices.

As the conversation progressed, Singayevsky blurted out that he
was under suspicion for the Yushchinsky murder. At that point,
Karayev broke off the conversation, as he wanted to make sure that
a third person, a witness, was present when Singayevsky "spills the
beans." At the next meeting, with Machalin on hand, Karayev
pointed to Singayevsky, saying, "There is the real murderer of
Yushchinsky—isn't it the way it happened?"

Singayevsky nodded, "Yes, it was our job." He went on to com-
plain that the "bastard's" body should have been thrown into the
Dnieper and not hidden in a cave so close to the Cheberyak home.
"Why did you leave so many footprints?" Karayev asked. "It was
the ministerial brain of Rudzinsky that planned it that way,"
Singayevsky replied.

At the trial, Singayevsky repudiated his confession and Karayev,
regarded by the prosecution as a "dangerous witness," was prevented from attending the trial for "security reasons."

Testimony of Sergei Machalin
October 10, 1913

PRESIDING JUDGE: Please tell us all you know about this case.
WITNESS: In September 1911, my friend Karayev and I became interested in this case. Permit me to give a profile of

Karayev. He is a graduate of a private educational institute; in 1902 he lived in the Caucasus and then in Odessa. In 1905 he arrived in Kiev and was arrested along with other persons. A search of his premises yielded weapons and explosives. While in detention, he experienced a toothache and requested permission to see a dentist. The prison warden ignored his request and derided him in front of the prisoners. Karayev vowed to avenge his treatment. Some time later, he again ran into the same warden and stabbed him to death. He was tried in front of a jury and was acquitted.

PROSECUTOR: Acquitted?

WITNESS: Yes, on this count he was acquitted, but was sentenced for possession of weapons and explosives. The incident with the warden aroused admiration among the prisoners, who considered him a hero. Thus, he never took his cap off when facing government authorities and never obeyed prison rules. His defiance of authority became widely known among the masses. To make him bow to authority, he was transferred to a maximum-security prison. Early in September 1911, I was his neighbor in a rundown section of Kiev, where I befriended and gave free lessons to the poor.

It was during this period that I became familiar with the Beilis case and its ritualistic overtones. Of course, the ritual aspect of this case was played up by the press, although official sources discounted this theory. A friend with whom I discussed this case posed the following question: "Listen, perhaps this is a ritual case; isn't it conceivable that the Jews do have such religious motives, justifying ritual murders?" I replied that this is "sheer nonsense; I don't believe in ritual murders and my conviction is well-founded." Yet, I saw that among the uneducated the belief in ritual murders was quite pronounced. However, when Beilis was implicated in what was described as a ritual murder, I thought to myself that the authorities apparently knew what they were doing, since they recognized that the detention of Beilis may trigger a pogrom in Kiev. At that point, I decided to devote more attention to this case.

When Brazul's first statement appeared in the press, I learned that professional thieves seemed to have had some connection to this case; among these, the name of Cheberyak had been frequently mentioned. From reading the Kiev press, I gained the impression that the evidence against Beilis was flimsy, to say the least. I had a nodding acquaintance with Brazul and decided to look him up, since he seemed to have a great deal of information on this case. Brazul was surprised to see me. He said: "Yes, I'm interested in this case, but my activities affected my health and sapped my strength . . . I therefore decided to drop it." My impression was that not knowing me well enough to trust me, he was trying to get rid of me. However, the thought that thieves were somehow involved in this case continued to trouble me and reinforced my resolve to ascertain the truth.

It was at this point that I decided to enlist my friend Karayev as a collaborator in this case. Karayev was in the Caucasus at that time, so I sent him a letter, asking him to return to Kiev, without disclosing the purpose of my request, but intimating that it might be worth his while. He arrived on the fifth of April. In the meantime, Brazul called on me unexpectedly, suggesting that I meet a certain person who was also interested in the Yushchinsky case. He assured me of that person's intelligence and integrity. Soon thereafter, Krasovsky came over, introducing himself as I. I. Karasev; he briefed me on the results of his findings and solicited my help in pursuing the investigation. Soon thereafter, Karayev arrived in Kiev. Since Vera Cheberyak and her circle of "friends" figured prominently in Krasovsky's briefing, I thought that Karayev—with his background and popularity with prison inmates—would be ideally suited to make contact with Cheberyak and her entourage. I proceeded to familiarize him with the case.

Karayev replied that he was wary to approach Cheberyak directly, inasmuch as she was under constant surveillance by the police. He said he knew a barber who was acquainted with Cheberyak's brother, Singayevsky, and could thus easily arrange a meeting with the latter. Such a meeting did take place. Karayev informed Singayevsky that he had accidentally learned that a warrant was issued for Singayevsky's arrest in connection with the Yushchisnky case. Singayevsky exploded in anger that that was all on account of the two "wenches"— the Dyakonov sisters. He rambled on in a state of extreme agitation, vowing first to break into the magistrate's office in order "to destroy the evidence," or alternately to kill Kirichenko, Colonel Ivanove, and the "damned sisters." I suggested that acting in haste would be counterproductive and offered our help, provided he filled us in on the details; my aim was to draw him out and have him reveal the circumstances of the murder and what the police authorities had on him and his cohorts. He said there wasn't much to tell. "We grabbed him and carried him to my sister's flat; suddenly the two wenches sauntered in. They didn't see a thing, but they saw us rushing out, which probably aroused their suspicion. As we ran out, we thought we ought to take a powder, but we had no money. The job we did at the Adamovich place yielded no money, only merchandise, which could not be easily disposed of. It was a terrible situation. Rudzinsky had but ten kopeks in his pocket, Latyshev came up with fifteen rubles, and I had ten rubles at home. With such a treasure trove we left for Moscow. We didn't take the merchandise along for fear of being apprehended on the way. We left it with Vera, and she was supposed to transfer it to Moscow. When the merchandise arrived, we started getting drunk. Latyshev pulled out a one-hundred-ruble bill and bellowed, 'Let's spend it all on booze.' A detective, sitting nearby, arrested Latyshev on the spot, and following a visit to the police station, shipped him back to Kiev."

PROSECUTOR: What's your occupation?

MACHALIN: I am preparing for a career in opera.

PROSECUTOR: I believe you testified that you were assisted financially by your family or someone else.

MACHALIN: That's correct. When I was in Kiev in March, my grandfather died; my grandfather had some property, and as administrator of the estate, I gained some income.

PROSECUTOR: Did you have anything to do with the secret police?

MACHALIN: No.

PROSECUTOR: Were you involved in politics? Were you interested in the Social Democratic Party?

MACHALIN: I was interested in social and political issues.

PROSECUTOR: I was referring to political affiliation.

MACHALIN: I was never officially involved.

PROSECUTOR: What do you mean by "officially involved"?

MACHALIN: I shared some of their views.

PROSECUTOR: Wasn't it politics that brought you together with Karayev, or did he interest you as a personality?

MACHALIN: When I settled in Kiev in September, Karayev lived nearby. I wanted to meet him as he aroused my curiosity. My interest stemmed from an item in the *Kievskaya Mysel* indicating that he was being accused of being a provocateur. I arranged to meet him, and following extensive conversations, I was persuaded that he was a highly decent person, although somewhat impulsive and holding definite leftist views. He asked me to convene an unofficial court composed of his closest friends to ascertain the reasons for the accusation against him.

PROSECUTOR: Members of the jury may not be familiar with the term "provocateur." Would you define it in a sentence or two?

MACHALIN: A provocateur is when one betrays his collaborators in, let us say, a crime.

PROSECUTOR: That is, one who joins their organization, familiarizes himself with its plans as an avowed sympathizer, and then betrays the participants to the authorities. Is that correct?

MACHALIN: It appears so.

PROSECUTOR: You said that the Yushchinsky case was of little interest to you, but when Brazul's declaration was publicized, it aroused your interest and prompted your involvement. When did Brazul make his declaration? Was it in January?

MACHALIN: Yes.

PROSECUTOR: You testified that when Beilis was implicated, you felt that there was hardly any evidence against him. You seem to have indicated that in the event Beilis was released, a pogrom against Jews would follow.

MACHALIN: I said that if the case is religiously motivated, the results would be the same. If he is acquitted, there will be a pogrom, as people will say, "The Yids used bribery"; if found guilty, a pogrom was still likely to follow.

ZAMISLOVSKI: You gave us a character profile of Karayev, but I'd like to know something about you. You said you studied at the Kharkov agricultural school. Did you graduate?

MACHALIN: No. In 1907, I was under investigation and was consequently dismissed from school.

ZAMISLOVSKI: Was that a secondary school?

MACHALIN: Yes.

ZAMISLOVSKI: What grade were you in when you were dismissed?

MACHALIN: Second.

ZAMISLOVSKI: Thus your education was rather skimpy?

MACHALIN: That's not for me to judge.

ZAMISLOVSKI: In 1907, you were seventeen years old.

MACHALIN: I think sixteen.

ZAMISLOVSKI: You were in second grade and were arrested on suspicion of expropriation?

MACHALIN: That's correct.

ZAMISLOVSKI: What was the nature of this expropriation?

PRESIDING JUDGE: This has no bearing on this case.

ZAMISLOVSKI: The law doesn't know of such a crime.

MACHALIN TO PRESIDING JUDGE: Your honor, I had no knowledge of this alleged expropriation. I was imprisoned, but there was no trial.

ZAMISLOVSKI: So you didn't know what you were imprisoned for. Was it forcible acquisition of money?

MACHALIN: Possibly.

ZAMISLOVSKI: So why don't you say that you were accused of robbery and were imprisoned for six months? Then you indicated that you were again arrested in 1908. How long were you in prison?

MACHALIN: Perhaps a month, or a month and a half.

ZAMISLOVSKI: Was that your last arrest?

MACHALIN: No. I was jailed last year.

ZAMISLOVSKI: Three times you were under arrest?

MACHALIN: Yes.

ZAMISLOVSKI: At the same time you testified that you did not belong to any political party.

MACHALIN: Yes.

ZAMISLOVSKI: Yet you intimated that you identified with a political program, or was it several such programs?

MACHALIN: This referred to Karayev.

ZAMISLOVSKI: How about you? Don't you identify with some views of the Socialist revolutionaries?

PRESIDING JUDGE: Witness is not obligated to answer that question.

MACHALIN: I refuse to answer.

ZAMISLOVSKI: So you refuse to respond to my question whether you share the views of the Social Revolutionary Party?

MACHALIN: At present, I am not implicated in any crime and am under no obligation to disclose my convictions.

ZAMISLOVSKI: So you summoned Karayev to come to Kiev. Did you offer to pay his expenses?

MACHALIN: No, I didn't. He apparently believed that the reason I invited him was something that concerned him personally.

ZAMISLOVSKI: You said you read something in the newspapers about Karayev, which was of a derogatory nature. Was he inferentially accused of being a provocateur?

MACHALIN: The sequence of events was as follows: Following the assassination of Stolypin, rumors abounded alleging the involvement of agents provocateurs, including Karayev. These rumors upset Karayev, and he was eager to ascertain the source of these allegations.

ZAMISLOVSKI: Now, let's throw some light upon the meetings you had with Karayev. At the first meeting, on the twenty-second, did you expect to find him in, or did you meet him by chance?

MACHALIN: It was entirely by chance.

ZAMISLOVSKI: Then you met him on the twenty-third and twenty-fourth. Was it on the twenty-fourth that Singayevsky had confessed?

MACHALIN: Yes.

SHMAKOV: You testified that the authorities pursued their investigation as if the crime was ritualistic, but you didn't share their opinion.

MACHALIN: I didn't believe it was ritualistic.

SHMAKOV: In other words, you ruled out the possibility that the murder was religiously motivated?

MACHALIN: I did not rule out the possibility that the crime was committed by Jews, but dismissed the ritualistic version.

SHMAKOV: On what grounds?

PRESIDING JUDGE: Mr. Shmakov, you pose questions as if the witness were an expert. Confine your questioning to facts.

SHMAKOV: Did you research this question? Was your conviction based upon perusing the Talmud?

MACHALIN: I based my belief on experience. If the government, the secret police, the detectives—sustained by public money—could not substantiate the existence of ritual murders, that meant they didn't exist.

PRESIDING JUDGE: Mr. Shmakov, you again question the witness as if he were an expert. I cannot allow this kind of interrogation.

SHMAKOV: Having dismissed the possibility of a ritual murder, you advanced the proposition that the crime might have been an act of revenge?

MACHALIN: I thought that Beilis might be involved, as I couldn't imagine that the authorities would arrest a person on frivolous grounds.

PRESIDING JUDGE: Please leave the authorities out of your conjectures.

SHMAKOV: You testified that your involvement in the investigation was prompted by the widespread interest this case had attracted in social circles. Where was the social interest?

MACHALIN: I already reported, rumors were rife in many parts of the country that the murder was of a religious nature and there was considerable agitation bordering on hysteria.

SHMAKOV: Rumors, the source of which was unknown to you?

MACHALIN: I could trace some of the sources. Some of my friends were affected by these rumors and agitation. Furthermore, the newspapers focused on this case, so it was hardly a secret.

SHMAKOV: And, on the basis of these suppositions and rumors, mostly anonymous, you sought to persuade Karayev to commit not an anonymous, but a concrete betrayal?

MACHALIN: The fact is, that at the tender age of thirteen or fourteen, I was an eyewitness to a pogrom in our townlet, Smela . . .

PRESIDING JUDGE: This has no connection with the case. Are you doing this to revive memories of 1904 or 1905?

SHMAKOV: Besides the evidence that you and your friends assembled against Singayevsky, was there any other data implicating Singayevsky?

MACHALIN: Not that I know of.

KARABCHEVSKY: From your testimony, I gathered that Karayev's political leanings may have been construed as criminal. Do you think he was a criminal?

MACHALIN: He may have been tried as a criminal, but in my eyes he was not a criminal.

KARABCHEVSKY: When you met Singayevsky and heard him talk, did he immediately impress you as a jailbird, using the vernacular of the underworld?

MACHALIN: Indeed, he did.

KARABCHEVSKY: Would you say he was a bright young man of average intelligence?

MACHALIN: No, he is a dimwitted, stupid man with very limited comprehension. Ask him a question, and you had to paint him a picture until he understood it.

KARABCHEVSKY: Did I understand you to imply that Brazul was a flighty, careless person? Did you confide in him, or did you keep your distance?

MACHALIN: Frankly speaking, I kept my distance; but inasmuch as he seemed to have had close relations with the authorities, I thought he might prove useful in case we ran afoul of the police.

GRUZENBERG: I gathered from your testimony that in the course of your conversations with Singayevsky, in which he had confessed his involvement in the crime, he expressed misgivings about the exposure of "two raspberries." What does it mean, the "exposure of two raspberries?"

MACHALIN: "Raspberries" refer to dens.

GRUZENBERG: Does it mean that on account of this case, two dens frequented by the underworld had been exposed?

MACHALIN: Yes.

GRUZENBERG: Do you know which specific dens he was referring to?

MACHALIN: I didn't care to ask.

GRUZENBERG: When you discussed the actual murder, didn't I hear you say that "Rudzinsky disposed of the body"?

MACHALIN: In the course of our conversation, while Karayev was trying to get Singayevsky to confess, he asked him, "Couldn't you find a better way to unload the body, burn it, or get rid of it somewhere?"; and Singayevsky replied, "It was the genius Rudzinsky who planned it that way."

GRUZENBERG: You also seemed to have made some references

to Latyshev, specifically that he threw up before or after the murder?

MACHALIN: Yes, I did question him about Latyshev, what type of a person he was, and he said, "Latyshev was a nice fellow, but he had no stomach for a 'wet' job."

GRUZENBERG: What does it mean, a "wet job"?

MACHALIN: That's a job that entails killing someone. And I said, "Why?" He answered, "He got real sick. He vomited."

GRUZENBERG: In response to a question by the prosecution, you said that you were arrested once for expropriation?

MACHALIN: Yes, I was.

GRUZENBERG: Was there a trial?

MACHALIN: No, the case was dismissed.

GRUZENBERG: What about the second time?

MACHALIN: This was a police inquest.

GRUZENBERG: And the third time?

MACHALIN: That was in 1912.

GRUZENBERG: Thereafter, you were arrested in July or August?

MACHALIN: It may have been in July, I don't recall precisely.

GRUZENBERG: What was the charge?

MACHALIN: The circumstances were as follows . . .

PRESIDING JUDGE: Was this a political case?

MACHALIN: No, I was arrested in connection with the Karayev case.

PRESIDING JUDGE: Hence it was a political case?

MACHALIN: No, no charges were brought against me.

GRUZENBERG: You were called to a hearing in May and in July and were detained in August in connection with the Karayev arrest?

PRESIDING JUDGE: Why do you persist in making a connection?

GRUZENBERG: I only pose questions. It is up to you and the jury to make connections.

MAKLAKOV: You said, that according to Singayevsky, Latyshev was unfit for a "wet job"?

MACHALIN: Yes.

MAKLAKOV: Are you aware what happened to Latyshev?

MACHALIN: Yes, he was questioned by the magistrate and when the latter brought up the Yushchinsky case, Latyshev made a dash for the window, hoping to slide down the water pipe, but he missed the pipe and plunged to his death.

MAKLAKOV: Last question: It was intimated to you that your and Karayev's behavior, vis à vis Singayevsky, constituted a form of entrapment, or at least an attempt to entrap?

MACHALIN: Yes.

MAKLAKOV: Were you persuaded that, had you failed to use this kind of entrapment, their misdeeds would be attributed to Beilis?

MACHALIN: Yes, I was convinced of this.

MAKLAKOV: Had Beilis not been implicated, and the whole matter revolved only about solving a crime, would you have behaved in the same manner?

MACHALIN: No, God forbid.

PROSECUTOR: If I understood you correctly, what Singayevsky's confession revealed was that they murdered the boy in the morning, committed a robbery in the evening, and left for Moscow the same night?

MACHALIN: No, they traveled to Moscow the following day.

PROSECUTOR: According to your scenario, they committed the murder and then transferred the body to the cave the same night. Were you interested in this question at all?

MACHALIN: Yes, that's the way it was. They tried to find the right site for the crime and hoped to lay their hands on some money for the trip, but the money did not materialize.

PROSECUTOR: Be that as it may, but the murder was executed in the morning, the robbery in the evening, and while totally absorbed in planning the robbery, they were simultaneously hard-pressed in obtaining the cash for the Moscow trip. Surely, they needed some time to carry out the boy's body, which in itself was an onerous task. With nosey neighbors around, how did they manage to transfer the body to the cave the same night and still depart for Moscow in the morning?

MACHALIN: I did not ascertain their movements that night.

PROSECUTOR: Did Krasovsky tell you that the Dyakonov sisters hypothesized that the body was transferred by other criminals, who did not participate in the murder?

MACHALIN: No, I was not aware of this.

7

O. V. Vipper's Closing
Argument for the
Prosecution

October 23, 1913

Members of the jury, as a prosecutor in this case, I carry a heavy responsibility, but your task may be even more onerous. For a whole month, you were deprived of your freedom, separated from your families and your normal occupations, sitting patiently in this stuffy hall and straining your senses to absorb the voluminous material brought to your attention. Your only reward is the recognition that you are serving the cause of justice and that your lips will ultimately pronounce the word that all of Russia is waiting for with mounting impatience—the word of truth. As you well know, this is a unique, unprecedented case. It was not too long ago that we experienced the torments of a revolution, which took a heavy toll in lives; people in government service had been mercilessly gunned down; Mother Russia was in the throes of a senseless bloodbath, and evil was rampant in the land. But even against this gruesome background, the murder of Yushchinsky stands out as an especially ghastly, unerasable stain.

In midday, in a large and ancient Russian city boasting of numerous sacred shrines and sites, an innocent boy, beloved by everyone, is suddenly seized, tortured, and repeatedly stabbed, his blood is drawn out, and his mutilated body thrown into a cave. Members of the jury, whoever committed this monstrous crime, Beilis or his collaborators, or some other evildoer, one cannot view this beastly deed with equanimity; and although young Andrey is a stranger to all of us, the circumstances of his death made him as one of our own. I could readily understand if the label of universality attached to this case was prompted by the barbarous nature of this murder. From this standpoint, this case deserves to be character- ized as a "world event." But the world is beset by other troubles, other concerns; insofar as the world is concerned, Andrey doesn't matter, and he'll soon be totally forgotten. The world is much more concerned with Beilis, and it is the interest in Beilis which makes this a "world trial." As soon as Beilis, a Jew, was implicated in this case, the whole world was aroused and a torrent of criticism and abuse was unleashed against Russia and its authorities—"How dare they indict a Jew in so heinous a crime?" Yet, Judaism is not on trial; we are dealing here with one Jew, who out of fanaticism or religious aberration, was moved to murder. Jews are, of course, afraid that if the Jew, Beilis, is convicted, it may provoke pogroms, and it may cast a pall of suspicion upon the entire Jewish nation. We know that pogroms usually afflict the poor and the disadvantaged Jews, while the leaders, who are responsible for this worldwide agitation, and who very often affront us with their surreptitious manipulations— these people are unaffected by pogroms.

We all recall the famous Dreyfus case, which aroused worldwide concern just because one Jew was accused of treason. Had the defendant been a non-Jew, say a Russian fanatic or pervert, would this case attract so much attention and turmoil? It is because Beilis is perceived to represent all of Jewry that the most famous lawyers had been engaged to defend him. Yet, let me make it perfectly clear—the Jewish people are not on trial here, and such words as "blood libel" bandied about in the press are totally inapplicable to this case. Nevertheless, as soon as the tortured body of the young

Yushchinsky was discovered, Jewish functionaries—not Beilis, for he is a person of limited means—unleashed a campaign to confound and becloud this case. And how correct was the expert Sikorsky, who pointed out how these movements in defense of Jews usually start. Every effort is made to mislead the investigating authorities, to steer the investigation off course and throw suspicion on others. It seems like a mysterious hand with access to untold riches was trying to entangle this case in a maze of harebrained allegations and wild conjectures to a point where investigators, working for two years, could not stumble onto the truth. In the end, we are compelled to sit here a whole month in order to unravel the knot.

But regardless of these strange detours in this investigation, we are inevitably propelled towards the Zaitsev estate where the crime was committed. As the accuser, my task is not only to prove the guilt of the defendant, Beilis, my assignment is somewhat more complex. I am duty bound to remove the stigma of guilt from the people who appeared before us as witnesses, who had been pilloried in the press as suspects, even as the real murderers. Members of the jury, you may have observed flashes of passion in the course of these proceedings—I don't deny it. But the law mandates for the government prosecutor to be dispassionate and calm, and I intend to be calm and detached. You will recall that the investigation in this case was assigned to the commander of the investigative branch of the police department, Mishchuk; this fellow was apparently a Judophile, who didn't believe that in the twentieth century there could be murders of a ritualistic nature. He thus subjected relatives to incredible cruelties and indignities on the basis of rumors and innuendoes generated primarily by staff members of *Kievskaya Mysel*, a newspaper that played a particularly meddlesome role in the investigation. The authorities soon realized that Mishchuk was getting rapidly nowhere and had him replaced with an experienced detective, Krasovsky, who comes to this case with a reputation as an able and skillful investigator.

Yet, even under the experienced Krasovsky a number of so-called suspects were rounded up only to be released for lack of

evidence. Strangely enough, these miscues can be attributed to the
efforts of several amateur sleuths—mostly of Jewish descent—associated with the newspaper *Kievskaya Mysel*, which task seemed to
have been to confound and mislead the investigating authorities.
Along the way, Krasovsky came up with the legend about switches;
this is, indeed, nothing more than a fairy tale, although the defense
had tried—vainly I believe—to give it a semblance of credibility.
The story is based on the incoherent testimony by an inebriated
woman—corroborated by an unidentified boy—who presumably
overheard a dispute between Zhenya Cheberyak and Andrey concerning switches. The boys apparently cut off some switches, Andrey's looked better than Zhenya's, and the latter coveted Andrey's
switch. The boys quarreled and exchanged verbal threats; Andrey
allegedly said that he would inform the authorities that Zhenya's
mother dealt in stolen goods, whereupon Zhenya countered
that he would tell Andrey's parents that he habitually skipped
school. Subsequently, so the legend spun, Andrey entered the
Cheberyak home, followed by two unidentified men, who said: "We
ought to get rid of him," and they presumably did. A veritable
goulash of rumors, hearsay, and plain nonsense. I must say in
defense of Krasovsky, that once the legend about the switches
evaporated into thin air, once the Prihodko "connection" was
demolished, Krasovsky finally found himself on the Zaitsev estate,
where he interviewed those living there, including Beilis.

Yet, even at this juncture, Krasovsky continued to play a duplicitous role. To Golubev he conceded the possibility of a ritual murder,
to others he dismissed it as a hoax. However, it was he who came up
with bits and pieces of evidence, which provided the groundwork
for implicating Beilis as a defendant in this case. He definitely
established that the crime was committed outside the cave, that
Andrey and Zhenya played near the brick factory's clay mixer, and
that they were frightened and chased away by Beilis, with the latter
seizing Andrey by the hand and dragging him toward the kiln.
Krasovsky said that Cheberyak maintained a close relationship with

Beilis, yet Beilis's son, Pinky, testified that he had never met Andrey and Zhenya, which was a transparent lie.

The same Krasovsky, who in conversations with different people, some of whom—witnesses in this case—seemed to have established a definite connection between Beilis and Cheberyak, expressed bewilderment when Beilis was arrested as a prime suspect, telling Brushkovsky: "What the hell is going on? They've arrested an innocent man." Thus, for one reason or another, Krasovsky had chosen to play a duplicitous role in these proceedings. Almost concurrently with Beilis's arrest, Cheberyak, too, was taken into custody as an alleged collaborator in the murder, since Krasovsky had never tired of insinuating that she is somehow involved in the boy's murder.

You've already heard the melancholy story how Cheberyak's only son, Zhenya, and subsequently her daughter, Valya, had succumbed to a sudden attack of dysentery and died shortly thereafter. We've heard some testimony which hinted that the children were poisoned. There is no factual evidence to substantiate this allegation, but I cannot overlook the fact that Krasovsky had surmised openly that Cheberyak may have had a hand in her children's death. This preposterous insinuation—of a mother poisoning her own children—prompts me to draw your attention to the persistent visits by detectives to the Cheberyak home, while the parents were absent, presumably to extract information from the children. The visiting sleuths usually came prepared to ply the children with sweets and pastries in order to make them talk. I am not suggesting that the detectives poisoned the children, yet the medical evidence in this episode remains inconclusive. One thing is certain: the official intruders frightened the children and used every devious trick to make them divulge what they knew; they obviously knew a great deal, as they were the last persons to see Yushchinsky alive.

Cheberyak also was extremely unnerved by the detectives, and as the testimony revealed, was reported to have prodded her son, Zhenya: "Tell them I had nothing to do with the murder." Yet, when the two children died, the surviving daughter, Ludmilla—at last relieved of the strain and tension generated by the detectives' constant prodding—had related in her testimony the circumstances of Yushchinsky's disappearance. Krasovsky, however, continued spinning the yarn about Cheberyak's complicity and about the involvement of her underworld co-conspirators. Having, at long last, cut a swathe to the Zaitsev estate and closing in on Beilis, he abruptly changed course and steered us once again toward Cheberyak and her shady friends. Whether Krasovsky's change of heart was prompted by Jewish pressure or for some other reasons, the celebrated detective was withdrawn from the case on the grounds of malfeasance in office.

Of course, the Jews find themselves in dire straits, and no one can deny it. Nevertheless, at the risk of being judged unfair by society, whose values I am trying to uphold, I feel impelled to say openly that I find myself under Jewish domination, that I am weighted down by the power of Jewish thought and the power of the Jewish press. For the Russian press is only marginally Russian; the fact is, that practically all organs of the print media are in Jewish hands. I don't want to speak against the Jews, but when one reads the Jewish press, Jewish publications, and Jewish defense organs, one cannot escape the conclusion that in criticizing them, one invites instant rebuke and disapproval. In doing so, you are either a reactionary, an obscurant, or a member of the Black Hundred. Having monopolized the press, they've become so arrogant as to believe that no one will dare to level such an accusation against them, not only in Russia, but in other countries as well. And to a certain degree, they are right. They have the wealth, and notwithstanding the fact that legally they possess few rights, they are in fact the rulers of our universe. In this respect, biblical prophesy may have been fulfilled; as bad as their condition admittedly is, we feel as being under their yoke.

I mention it because no one thought that our government would take the risk of bringing this case to trial. Yet surely we could not close our eyes to the dastardly crime that was committed in Kiev.

One would think that Jewish society, believing as it apparently does in the judicial system, would react calmly to these proceedings, letting the judicial process take its course. But no, the accusation against one of their own stunned them. Instead of following these proceedings rationally and dispassionately, they conspired to confound and confuse the investigation of this case, presumably because they believe that Beilis is guilty. Once Beilis was implicated, they proceeded—in a mercenary way—to befuddle and lead astray the investigating authorities. The first to emerge on the scene was Brazul-Brushkovsky, of the newspaper *Kievskaya Mysel*, a non-Jew, but married to a Jewess, who volunteered his services in the investigation, ostensibly in the interests of justice, but, in fact, for self-promotion and material gain.

Then we are confronted with Margolin, who proudly proclaimed that he represented the Jewish community, a lawyer who purports to handle the community's major lawsuits. They soon inveigle Krasovsky to join their intimate circle, and together they devise a plan designed to mislead and misdirect the investigation.

Brazul comes with an announcement to the court prosecutor, declaring that he had followed the sequence of events in the Yushchinsky murder from the very beginning and has come to the conclusion that the murder was the work of a gang of criminals who sought to simulate a ritual murder, and thus cover their tracks. The prosecutor was not persuaded to order a new investigation on the basis of Brazul's unsolicited declaration, but Brazul—undeterred—decided "to shift gears" and seek other ways to mislead the authorities. He then engineered the mysterious pilgrimage to Kharkov, where Vera Cheberyak was to meet, not once but twice, the "distinguished gentleman," purportedly a member of the Imperial Duma, Mr. Margolin. The details of the Kharkov trip have not been fully ascertained, owing to the contradictory versions offered by Brazul and Cheberyak, but Margolin conceded that it was—for him at least—a risky indiscretion, which may have exposed him to criminal proceedings. Krasovsky, as you know, was removed from his post in January, but he continued to operate as a private investigator in order, as he claimed, "to rehabilitate" himself. To assist him in restoring his good name, he enlisted the services of Karayev and Machalin, whose propensities for revolutionary and other illicit activities led them in and out of prison with undeviating regularity. Karayev was, of course, a more colorful personality with a reputation for fearlessness, a man who stabbed to death a prison official who had the temerity to scoff at Karayev's discomfort as a result of a toothache. Whether Karayev is a provocateur, as had been alleged, is not for us to decide, but there is no question of his impulsive, indeed, explosive temperament. Machalin, in contrast, is a good-looking young man with manners to match, possessed of a well-modulated voice (after all, he was preparing for a career in opera) and a good vocabulary; yet, isn't his exterior a sham? Isn't he just a good, smooth-talking, shrewd actor, familiar with the mores of the underworld, who managed to outwit and entrap the dimwitted Singayevsky?

So Krasovsky, with his newfound associates, whose prison experience had apparently refined their propensities for entrapment and betrayal, proceeded to concoct a plan targeting Vera Cheberyak as the central figure in the Yushchinsky murder. To achieve this, they first sought to ascertain who of Cheberyak's friends were in Kiev on or around March twelfth, so as to "work them over" and, perhaps, extract a confession. Secondly, they proceeded to corral a couple of witnesses, who were prepared to testify that when entering Cheberyak's flat they found the place in disarray; they then needed someone like Mrs. Malitsky, a chronic liar, who was ready to confirm the testimony of the Dyakonov sisters. Their aim was so to entangle the case as to warrant a new investigation.

I have already established that Rudzinsky, Latyshev, and Singayevsky were present in Kiev on March twelfth. On that same day, they took part in a robbery and traveled to Moscow. How could they have participated in a murder when they were busy perpetrating a robbery on the same day? Who would carry out the body? Surely, not Cheberyak and her children. A highly unlikely scenario. It has been suggested that Cheberyak had other associates, such as

Mandzelevsky and Mosiak, who could have handled the transfer of the body. Yet the record showed that from March tenth to March fourteenth, the above named had been in prison. What else do we have? Well, we have the Dyakonov sisters, who amused us with their hallucinations about a masked phantom supposedly trailing them, and whose other testimony was equally fictitious.

What is not fictitious, but a matter of historic record, is that ritual murders did occur and the circumstances in those cases strongly resembled some of the features of the case before us.

In the Saratov case, for instance, three Jews and some Christians were implicated in a ritual crime. Three Jews were under suspicion and a few Christians were sent to Siberia for resettlement.

In that case, two Christian boys were repeatedly stabbed to death and their blood was drawn out . . .

KARABCHEVSKY: There was nothing of the kind.

PRESIDING JUDGE: It was subsequently established that no ritual murder took place.

PROSECUTOR: Be that as it may, but two bottles of blood were sent to the Lubavitch rabbi, who, as you will recall, was none other than Shneerson.

Members of the jury, I trust that in your deliberations you will not erase from your memory the image of the martyred boy, Yushchinsky. Let Beilis be deemed innocent by the Jewish people, even the whole world; to Russians, Beilis is no saint. If he is convicted, Russia will try to forget this sordid episode associated with his name. But Beilis's name should never be allowed to dim the luminous image of Yushchinsky, whose tortured death touched a responsive chord in every Russian's heart. You cannot, will not, I am sure, shrink from the duty of pronouncing sentence upon this fanatic; Russia looks to you for an affirmative sentence. I trust you will summon the courage and fortitude to convict the defendant . . . and may Almighty God be your guide.

8

V. A. Maklakov's Closing Argument for the Defense

October 25, 1913

Members of the jury, we are told that the whole world's attention is focused on this trial. I would like to forget the world's interest, as it is your attention that is essential to bring this trial to a just conclusion. The prosecutor told you—and that's true—that a great deal of passion has been injected into these proceedings; but I've been calm and hope to remain so. For the question that seems to agitate the world is not focused on Yushchinsky, not even on Beilis, but on an ancient problem, namely, is it true or not that Jewish books, Jewish teachings—both ancient and contemporary—encourage the use of human blood. What is it—a covenant of blood that the Jews managed to conceal for centuries, or is it simply a fairy tale? I don't want to grapple with this problem, nor do I believe that you, members of the jury, can in good conscience undertake to resolve this question. May God give you the wisdom to resolve only the question of the Yushchinsky murder without delving into what even the prosecutor conceded may be an ancient myth. We know that in the Middle Ages witches were burned at the stake, people were tortured to extract a "confession."

The task before you is much simpler: a crime has been committed, a brutal, beastly crime, the perpetrator has not been found, the murderer is being sought. The prosecutor and the civil prosecutors think that they've found the criminal. They claim that the guilty man is Beilis. If they say they are convinced of Beilis's guilt, I have to believe them, although I seriously question their judgment. Whether Beilis or someone else committed the crime rests—in the final analysis—on your judgment, and the task of the prosecution and the defense is to help you arrive at a fair and just decision. We can help you sift through this maze of evidence, if we remain calm and dispassionate. The prosecutor understood this. Indeed, he promised to be calm and unemotional, but he didn't keep his promise. He said that the trial stirred him to outrage and indignation; and, indeed, his sense of outrage has been reflected in his tone and gestures. My reaction is that outrage and indignation in this case are dangerous and superfluous. Surely, if you've uncovered the culprits, if you know who perpetrated the crime, then indignation is useless, since the killer of Yushchinsky will deserve no mercy and the prosecution's task will be an easy one. I know of no defenders who would undertake to defend this senseless murderer. However, if the killer has not been found, it's incumbent upon us to find him. You are being pulled in all directions; you are being confused. I said that passion and indignation are dangerous things in these proceedings, as they tend to confuse rather than convince. Indignation led the prosecutors to expand their accusations to include a whole nation.

They said that they are not accusing the Jewish people as such; but what did the prosecutor say about Jewish customs, the power of Jewish money, the cabal of the Jewish press and Jewish society, all of whom contrived to confound this case? The civil prosecutor has chosen to lump together excerpts from the Talmud, which are alien to most Jews, with historical events antedating the birth of Christ, and reaching the conclusion that Jews abhor Christian people. In doing so, he even indicted Beilis's children, who—according to one testimony—were laughing at the sight of Yushchinsky being dragged toward the kiln. However, the prosecutor apparently had a lapse of memory, as the testimony in question, that of Vassily Cheberyak, quoting Zhenya Cheberyak's alleged story, recited how Yushchinsky, having broken loose from Beilis's grip, was running away with Beilis in pursuit. Not a word about Yushchinsky being dragged somewhere. Isn't this a familiar sight when children play? A boy running, an adult chasing—a scene evoking merriment and laughter. Why did the prosecutor choose to dredge up this scene? The conclusion seems obvious—Jewish children are trained from early age to despise Christians and scoff at Christian misadventures; hence, the derisive laughter by Beilis's children. Anyone who can deduce a malevolent intent from such a simple, innocent child's play is making a mockery of truth and loses all claim to credibility.

There are people who hate Jews for a variety of reasons. They despise the rich Jews and the poor Jews, the privileged and the disadvantaged. Such people are disqualified from judging Jews, such people cannot be fair and just, and their judgment cannot be trusted. There are moments when hate corrodes the mind and hardens one's conscience. Pogroms against Jews have been frequently brought up in these proceedings, but the indiscriminate assaults against Jews invariably arouse feelings of indignation and remorse among the people of Russia. Yet pogroms, however repugnant, are one thing; but here is a court of justice, here you are sworn to uphold the law—not to convict the innocent—here you are honor bound to be fair to the exclusion of all extraneous considerations.

We are faced with a choice: either we seek to uncover the truth, or we are hell-bent to offer a sacrifice in memory of Yushchinsky. If we want to make sure that the guilty should not escape punishment, then you, members of the jury, must be dispassionate and considerate. Your task is less onerous than that of the prosecution. You are not obligated to find the guilty; this is not your responsibility. That's the responsibility of the prosecution. Armed with all the power and resources of government, theirs is the task to apprehend the guilty. Once they believe that they've found him, once they've assembled all the evidence available to them, they come before you and say:

"We are not the judges; it is conceivable that we're wrong. We think we found the guilty one—here is everything we have against him. If you're satisfied that the evidence is sufficiently persuasive, say so; however, if you think otherwise, tell the authorities to continue the search for other evidence, other possible culprits. It will not be your fault if the crime is unsolved, if the murder is not avenged."

If this case were conducted in accordance with normal procedures, the prosecution would have come to you and said: "Here is the evidence against Beilis. Tell us, are we mistaken or not?" And the trial would have been over long ago. Yet, in this case, the prosecution had chosen to follow a different course. It laid out before you the full story: who were the early suspects and who was implicated later, how the search was conducted and how it was misdirected. Included in this tortuous story were shreds of evidence against Beilis. I am afraid that this method may lead you into what is known as an "optical deception." Through a process of elimination, the accusers first absolved all those who initially figured as prime suspects. "Surely," argued the prosecution, "if Prihodko is not guilty, if Nezhinsky is not guilty, if Cheberyak is not guilty, the culprit must be Beilis, even if the evidence against him is almost nonexistent." One civil prosecutor gave the question a different twist: "It has to be either Beilis or Cheberyak, perhaps both of them;" and then he went on to say, "Once Beilis is convicted, the authorities would then proceed to implicate others, including Cheberyak, but if you free Beilis, the search for others will cease."

I've heard many strange things in the course of this trial, but this maneuver of convicting one in order—through him—to apprehend another, that's unheard of in the annals of justice.

You will recall that all the evidence against Beilis is based on Cheberyak's testimony. Once you decide that her testimony is not credible, the case against Beilis disintegrates.

The prosecutor referred to the volunteer investigators, the amateur sleuths, who for reasons of self-promotion, undertook to solve this case in their own way, and have indeed thrown this case into total disarray by their meddlesome, gratuitous activities. Brazul-

Brushkovsky, the resourceful journalist with easy access to the authorities, was anxious to solve this case all by himself and thus become a celebrity with a substantial increase in pay, and Barschevsky, a lesser light in the journalistic firmament, who sought to throw suspicion on Yushchinsky's mother because she was dry-eyed when reporting her son's disappearance. This student of human nature couldn't see the anguish in the mother's eyes because she wasn't crying. These two have so confused our helpless and inept authorities that they have fully earned the gratitude of the prosecution.

But the accusers, the distinguished members of the prosecution, have not been honest and forthcoming; instead of characterizing these meddlers as troublesome do-gooders seeking self-glorification, the prosecutors took pains to portray them as agents of a deliberate Jewish conspiracy designed to lead astray the investigating authorities. This is a nightmarish scenario, as irrational as it is incredible.

Take the case of Brushkovsky and his cohorts. This worldly, sophisticated journalist and man-about-town latched on to Vera Cheberyak in order to get her to talk about her underworld connections, which—he felt—would give him the clue to Yushchinsky's murder. What transpired, however, was that this shrewd, streetwise woman led them by the nose, outwitting them at every opportunity. Ponder the strange trip to Kharkov, where Brushkovsky introduced Cheberyak to a "distinguished gentleman," who turned out to be the attorney and Jewish communal leader, Margolin. What did the Cheberyak woman tell us about this encounter? With a straight face, she said Margolin had offered her 40,000 rubles for taking the murder of Yushchinsky upon herself.

Members of the jury, don't you see that this woman, who is so adept at skirting the truth, finally tripped herself up with this whopper? If she had been offered 40,000 rubles for keeping her mouth shut about what she knew about Beilis, or for laying the blame on her erstwhile lover, Miffle, her version about the bribe might have been believable. But taking the blame for murder—a grisly, ghastly murder—for 40,000 or 400,000 rubles—why, this is sheer madness!

The prosecutors have seen fit to vent their righteous indignation upon the amateur investigators, the meddlers, who out of sheer stupidity or naiveté had befuddled our primitive, even inept, system of investigation. After all, that's why Beilis is the defendant in this case! But the prosecution must show a sense of fairness. The accusers had meddlesome volunteers serving their cause, too. When I saw before us members of the Double-Headed Eagle, I knew that these people would not bring us closer to the truth, because they were absolutely certain that they knew the truth already. They were convinced that ritual murders do exist, hence, the culprit must be Beilis. Brazul-Brushkovsky and his companions have had easy access to the investigating authorities, but Golubev had no trouble seeing the highest court officials in their offices, even homes. Golubev, it seems, had political clout, as he was undoubtedly responsible for Mishchuk's removal from the case simply because he had dismissed the notion of ritual murders as "foolishness." When I asked Razmitalsky, the official who gave Mishchuk his walking papers, whether he had the authority to dismiss a ranking police official, he replied that he had consulted with "higher-ups," including members of the Imperial Duma, who approved his action. Here we clearly see the heavy-handed intrusion of the political establishment into these proceedings. When Krasovsky was appointed to succeed Mishchuk, he, too, was closely supervised by the political "higher-ups," and when his findings did not measure up to their expectations, he was similarly dismissed and discredited.

Members of the jury, if there is a scintilla of truth that has surfaced time and time again in these proceedings, it is the complicity of Vera Cheberyak in Andrey's murder. I'm not saying that she was an active participant, but that she knows who killed the boy is no longer in doubt. The prosecutor intimated that Cheberyak's involvement in the crime does not vindicate Beilis, suggesting that once Beilis is convicted, Cheberyak will be "next in line." You will recall that Cheberyak had been a suspect all along, had been arrested numerous times. Why is she keeping quiet? Why doesn't she lash out against the police who pursued her, badgered and harassed her, gave her no peace? She could have said: "Leave me alone, it was Beilis who dragged Andrey to the kiln," but her lips are sealed.

Krasovsky hinted that she might have poisoned her children, and she, in turn, retaliated by suggesting that it was Krasovsky and his agents who may have had a hand in their demise.

It is abundantly clear that both of them are not telling the truth, since the medical evidence had ruled out poison as the cause of death. It is simply inconceivable that a mother, any mother, would poison her own child. However, Cheberyak's behavior in rushing to the hospital—on being told her son was gravely ill—and dragging the ailing boy all through town, so he could "die at home," as she told us, is the behavior of a woman in a state of extreme fear or panic. She knew that her son would get better care in the hospital, but she rushed him home. Why? She was afraid that the feverish boy might blurt out something to the detectives hovering nearby, a word, a sentence that would sink her, that would link her to the Yushchinsky murder.

You remember how she warned her son—with all kinds of threatening gestures—to keep his mouth shut? Yet her natural love for her son gave way to a paroxysm of fear that Zhenya, in his agony, might reveal her complicity in Andrey's murder. And when Zhenya, in the throes of death, cried out, "Mama, leave me in peace, I'm in pain," the grieving mother proceeded to kiss him on the mouth, giving him the Judas kiss to smother his mouth, lest he blurt out the truth.

Vera Cheberyak was weeping when she told us about her son's death, and I can readily understand her torment and her anguish. Yet, if Yushchinsky's death calls for retribution, his blood was partially avenged by this woman's unredeemed grief.

What has transpired in this case is, frankly, bewildering. Cheberyak has been under suspicion right from the start, she has been jailed numerous times, but the investigating officials kept releasing her. Instead of holding on to that thread in order to

unravel the tangled skein, instead of keeping her under close surveillance and monitoring her every move, she was led to believe that
she was immune from prosecution. Why? Because the authorities
were inclined to pursue other leads, to move in a different direction.

One of our adversaries, Shmakov, intimated that Cheberyak, too,
might have been seduced by Jewish money. If that is so, why don't
you press her to reveal her Jewish co-conspirators?

It's sheer insanity to conclude that the Jews would place themselves at risk by putting their trust in this wily, slippery woman. The
fact is that Cheberyak's accomplices are to be found somewhere
else, beyond the walls of this hall, beyond the dock of the accused.
Once the government prosecutors decided that the culprit is Beilis,
they studiously dismissed all evidence to the contrary as "garbage,"
and in a display of outright bias or official myopia, branded all
witnesses that didn't toe the line as perjurers.

Let's refresh our memory about the erratic record of the investigation. There were hairs on Andrey's body when discovered. The
authorities took samples of hair from Beilis—from every part of his
body. But did they take similar hair samples from Rudzinsky,
Latyshev, and Singayevsky? No, they did not, presumably fearful of
what they may reveal. There were some traces of clay on Andrey's
clothing. The authorities tried to match them with samples of clay
taken from the Zaitsev estate, and the tests, admittedly, were
inconclusive. Why didn't they take clay samples from Cheberyak's
basement, where the boy's body may have been kept? No explanation. Then, there was the carpet in Cheberyak's flat, which, on
inspection, revealed some suspicious spots, possibly blood spots.
The officials cut out a few fibers from the carpet for further scrutiny.
Why just a few fibers? Why didn't they take the whole carpet for a
thoroughgoing examination? Apparently saving Cheberyak's "precious" carpet was more important than saving a life. Members of the
jury, isn't it obvious that the authorities simply refused to hold on to
the thread for fear that it may lead them in the direction they did not
choose to move?

The prosecution heaped scorn upon Karayev, branding him a

"provocateur," an outlaw, a perjurer. Why didn't the prosecution produce him as a witness so that he could be cross-examined, so that his veracity could be tested? It was precisely a person of Mr. Karayev's background—a political rebel, a man who refused to kowtow to the authorities, thus acquiring an underworld reputation of a fearless nonconformist and a hero—that was needed to establish contact with Cheberyak's friends and gain their confidence; and that's exactly what he did, extracting a confession from Singayevsky. The fact that Karayev had a long prison record did not automatically disqualify him as a credible witness. After all, he didn't receive or ask for a monetary reward for traveling all the way from Caucasus to be of service in this case. He did it voluntarily, knowing full well that he risked being detained and imprisoned by the police, who had him under constant surveillance. In any event, Karayev and Machalin, in inducing Singayevsky to confess to the murder, did not commit a provocation, as the prosecution had claimed. If they used devious means to set Singayevsky up, such as telling him a few lies and plying him with vodka, such tactics are routinely used by our secret services.

There was a tense, dramatic moment when Machalin and Singayevsky confronted each other. You will recall the scene when Machalin looked Singayevsky straight in the eye and the latter averted his gaze, obviously discomfited by Machalin's relentless stare. For a moment—a long, agonizing moment—it seemed to me as if Singayevsky was ready to blurt out a confession; but that was not to be, as the prosecutor came to his rescue. "I have several questions for this witness," the prosecutor interjected. We protested the intrusion, but the spell was broken, the promising opportunity was allowed to slip away.

What evidence did the prosecution assemble against Beilis? Why is he on trial? We are told that there was a premeditated plan to lure Andrey into the Zaitsev estate to consummate a sacrificial rite. According to Cheberyak, who was allegedly so informed by Zhenya and her little daughter, a group of children, including Andrey, traipsed over into the factory grounds to ride the clay mixer and

suddenly—in front of everyone present—Beilis grabbed Andrey and
dragged him toward the kiln. All the other children fled except for
Andrey, who was prevented from escaping. Surely, even the accusers must realize the flimsiness of this scenario; if it was a carefully conceived plan involving visiting Jewish clerics from foreign
countries, why was it timed to take place in the light of day with so
many witnesses watching? Suppose the children had changed their
mind and proceeded to a different site to while away their time? In
that case, the solemn religious rite of a sacrificial offering would
have been aborted and the carefully laid plans would have gone
awry. How can anyone believe this fairy tale? This is as ludicrous as
the Cheberyak-concocted yarn about the 40,000 rubles. Andrey's
abduction, said Cheberyak, was quite simple: he was seized and
dragged to the kiln, while all the children were watching. Surely,
the whole street would have been up in arms once the children
reported the abduction to their parents and friends. The fact of the
matter is that the whole incident never occurred and the abduction
never took place. The whole episode was a figment of Cheberyak's
skewed imagination.

The accusers claim that everyone had been corrupted by Jewish
money—the children, their parents, the whole neighborhood had
been silenced, immobilized by the Jewish colossus. Do you believe
it?

The prosecution questioned the credibility of Machalin and
Karayev on account of their "revolutionary" propensities, but said
nary a word about the police informer Kazachenko. The latter, as
you will recall, was Beilis's cell mate in prison who cozied up to
Beilis to gain his confidence. Beilis trusted him and gave him a letter
to deliver to his wife. When freed from jail, Kazachenko passed
the letter on to the jail warden. Colonel Ivanove referred to
Kazachenko as a man who told the truth only on rare occasions.
Yet, what did the letter say? It asked Beilis's wife to find the
perjurers who are out "to get him." A natural request from one who
knows he is innocent. Yet the prosecutors seized upon the compro-
mising part of the letter, in which he allegedly advised his wife to

give Kazachenko money so he would arrange to poison the "Frog" and the "Lamplighter." However, Nakonechny, nicknamed "the Frog," and Schachovsky, the Lamplighter, have both testified against Cheberyak and in favor of Beilis—so why poison them? Kazachenko apparently picked up bits and pieces of information about this case, but didn't have enough sense to digest it. As the Russian proverb goes, "He heard the tinkling of a bell, but where it came from he couldn't tell." So much for this paragon of truth and virtue.

The accusations against Beilis are nothing but a bizarre patchwork of coincidences. A "strange coincidence," argued the prosecutor, that on March twelfth, the date of Andrey's murder, Shneerson moved out of the Zaitsev estate. Mr. Shmakov rose to his feet to correct the prosecutor: "I rise to correct the statement of my colleague, the prosecutor, Shneerson did not move out, but moved in on March twelfth." Our adversaries are not easily assuaged—"he moved in" is evidence, "he moved out" is also evidence. This reminds me of the question Mr. Shmakov addressed to the medical experts: whether the murderers had a knowledge of anatomy. According to Mr. Shmakov's reasoning, if they hit the vein, they knew anatomy, if they did not, they also knew anatomy. The prosecutor claims that this was a meticulously planned ritual murder, conceived well in advance to take place on a given date— March twelfth—so as to allow a whole assortment of religious functionaries from abroad to be on hand to witness the ceremony. Suddenly, Shneerson picks the same date—March twelfth—to move in or out of the Zaitsev estate. Was that particular date chosen to conform to some ritual? Expert Pranaitis did not mention the date, and Neophite did not refer to it in his writings. If this was a coincidence, so be it, but it's certainly not evidence.

Another strange coincidence. Two unknown Jews chased some dogs away from their premises. Following this incident, the dogs died. This, we're told, is not a coincidence; there's something "fishy" about the dogs' sudden demise What was it then? A religiously inspired act of Jewish revenge? At long last, the accusers promised that they would hereafter dwell on Beilis's personality. So what did they disclose? That Beilis was a religious fanatic, that he displayed strange traits of behavior? None of that. The only thing they came up with was that Beilis, as a trustworthy employee, was instructed to deliver matzos to Zaitsev's kinsmen.

Is this the profile of a fanatic? The fact is that Beilis was a hard worker, a clerk doing his chores, doing what his employer tells him to do and nothing more. Having adduced no evidence against him, the prosecutor dredged up another "clue." "Look how he behaves himself in court . . . when asked whether he was a Jew, he replied with undisguised pride, 'Yes, I am a Jew.' " No one but the prosecutor's sensitive ear could have captured "the pride" in Beilis's voice. Of course, when a man is deprived of his freedom for two and a half years, accused of a beastly crime allegedly motivated by his religious beliefs, his emphatic response reflected, I believe, not ethnic arrogance, but a simple repudiation of a religious libel. The prosecutor then made a few choice comments about Beilis's smugness and self-control, presumably untouched by the grisly recital of Andrey's murder. "He only cried once throughout these proceedings," thundered the prosecutor. But the accuser never bothered to inquire about Beilis's state of health, his sickly pallor, which is symptomatic of acute anemia; and when Beilis fainted, the prosecutor sought to interpret it as an indication of guilt. Yet when Golubev, one of the prosecutor's main witnesses, collapsed on the witness stand, the prosecutor had no comment.

What else is there to implicate Beilis? There being no evidence against the accused, the prosecution attempts to indict an entire nation. Experts were summoned to prove that a ritual murder has been committed. One can understand the need for experts once the prosecution had proven Beilis's complicity in the murder and if its case were based on solid evidence and not on the convoluted testimony of Vera Cheberyak. Had that been established, experts could certainly throw some light on the state of mind and motives of the murderer. But the so-called experts, when questioned about the source of their testimony, could not produce one credible book or text for verification. Surely, a case which attracted worldwide attention deserves experts of unimpeachable scholarly credentials. Instead, we've heard excerpts from the scholarly works of the monk Neophite, who, as the prosecutor told us, had acquired his information from his father. I will quote only three segments from the book, as recorded by the court reporter, dealing with certain secrets of Jewish practice and behavior. Thus Neophite revealed in his book that European Jews have sores on their buttocks, the African Jews suffer from boils, etc. etc. He further disclosed that four times a year drops of blood fall on Jewish food, and when the blood dries, the food becomes toxic and anyone eating it dies. Another disclosure states that on a particular evening once a year all Jews go out of their minds. What is this, the prattle of an unhinged ignoramus, or an acute manifestation of senility?

This is the type of scholarly expertise relied upon by the prosecution in order to indict Beilis. Fortunately, our courts rarely, if ever, tolerate or admit such expert testimony.

Then we have the testimony of two other unknown clerics who sincerely believe in the existence of ritual murders. They too have no firsthand knowledge of the matter, but have heard it whispered in their sheltered monasteries.

The expertise of Professor Sikorsky was even more perplexing. As a rule, I have learned to respect dissenting opinions, but the esteemed professor seemed to have misunderstood why he was invited here. He was called here as an expert in psychology, but his testimony touched on matters totally unrelated to psychology. Not only did he disagree with the other medical experts, he even refused to communicate with them. Instead of offering us an opinion based on science, he rattled off a list of court cases linked to ritual murders, which knowledge he had gained from reading books in French and other languages. When asked to name his sources, he declined. In fact, his testimony was all hearsay and unsubstantiated allegations totally unrelated to psychiatry. What else do we have, besides the psychiatric evaluation, which much to our chagrin was nothing but a tedious detour into the realm of ritual murders? Of course, we still have the medical expertise to ponder upon. One of the most confusing and incomprehensible aspects of this trial was precisely the medical experts.

How did the official indictment portray the murder? The boy was pounced upon, undressed with only his cap left on his head, and his hands tied behind his back. Then came the blows, many blows administered by a trained hand with the sole aim of extracting all the blood. The indictment clearly indicated that the perpetrators had a basic knowledge of anatomy. Yet what transpired in this case was something that often occurs when truth bursts forth in spite of all attempts to suppress it. What the medical experts revealed was that the description of the murder as recorded in the indictment was false. To start with, the boy's hands were not tied behind his back before the assault; they were tied after he was dead. Thus the first blows landed when the boy was dressed, with blood spurting out onto his jacket and his shirt. Only later was he undressed. This brings us to the myth of the killers' familiarity with the human anatomy. Had the killer or killers known anything about anatomy, determined as they were to obtain as much blood as possible, why didn't they aim their blows so as to sever a vein? Not one vein was touched in the indiscriminate assault.

Thus the gruesome scenario envisaged by the prosecution—of a trained ritual slaughterer, adept in anatomy, removing the boy's cap and jacket and proceeding to put him to death with carefully targeted blows—has been decisively demolished by the medical experts.

Members of the jury, if this was a ritual murder, witnessed by a *tzadik*, with special containers on hand to accumulate the precious liquid, the boy would have been undressed and his hands tied prior to the assault. What actually happened was that the blood flowed freely, soaking up his shirt and jacket, the blows were administered indiscriminately with a dull instrument totally unsuitable for what was described as a premeditated, carefully planned religious exercise.

As I see it, Andrey was put to death in the following manner: Getting together in Cheberyak's flat, the "troika" of thieves has been contemplating their unenviable position. "We're caught up in a cycle, which bodes ill for all of us," they ruminated. "All of us are facing imminent arrest as a result of the Adamovich break-in . . . somebody is tattling, someone is betraying us . . ." At that point, Andrey appears, looking for Zhenya. Initially, the troika may not have had murder in their minds, but the boy's appearance probably triggered the thought that he may well have been the "squealer" and the source of their distressing predicament. Bear in mind that these men were savages, ready to pounce upon anyone at the slightest provocation. Andrey was a convenient target for their frustrations. Since Andrey did not bother to remove his cap, one of the hoodlums knocked the cap off the boy's head with such ferocious vehemence that blood spurted out from head and face and he may have lost consciousness. The boy probably cried out, so he was gagged for fear that his cry might alarm the neighbors below. The troika continued to pummel the boy, having made the decision "to finish him off." Now, the killers were in a quandary: "What to do with the body? Let's put him in the bathtub or some other place."

I'm ready to conclude. The evidence against Beilis, having been completely discredited and demolished, the prosecution nevertheless persists in defending Cheberyak, treating her with kid gloves. Judicial proceedings are not infallible; quite often, the guilty escape prosecution, as we're all human, bereft of divine guidance. There are occasions when we convict the innocent. When that occurs as a result of circumstantial evidence that is persuasive and compelling, evidence that even the sensitive conscience of twelve judges cannot disregard, we then have what is known as a judicial error, for which our judicial system cannot be blamed. But when we see the real culprits being sheltered, when we see a man being judged on the basis of the testimony of such a reliable, "honest" witness as Cheberyak, or the "scholarly" expertise of the monk Neophite, we cannot in good conscience conclude that this was the result of an honest judicial error.

I ask myself, why and how did all this come about? I cannot lead myself to believe that it was the enmity against Jews, which permeated these proceedings, that is likely to influence the outcome of this case. I simply refuse to believe it. I couldn't understand the thrust of

the indictment against Beilis until the prosecutor and his associates
came up with the answer. I'm glad they didn't mince words so that
our response can be equally forthright and unmistakable.

You were told that this case was unique, and that it does not
revolve around the fate of a poor clerk named Beilis; you were told
that the stakes in this case are much higher. The prosecutor was
quite specific: "The Jews felt that the investigating authorities
would not dare to initiate this case," and again, "It was the code of
the Jewish people and its ringleaders that is responsible." There you
have the explanation. There you have the "optical deception" I told
you about.

Behind Beilis's back, another global drama was being staged, a
drama with sinister overtones for the entire Jewish people. This
represents a grievous blow to our judicial system. You, members of
the jury, are duty bound to rise above the passions generated in this
courtroom. If we seek a fair, a just verdict, we must realize that all
the errors—real or imaginary—inherent in Jewish customs and
beliefs, or that had been committed by the Jewish people, have
absolutely nothing to do with Beilis. If you believe that you are
being called upon to judge Beilis, who sits here helpless, confronting
the immense power of the government; if you believe that you've
been summoned to pass judgment upon a worldwide Jewish conspiracy rooted in antiquity, then your verdict cannot be consistent
with the truth; as the victim will not only be Beilis, but the Russian
sense of justice, indeed, our entire judicial system. Beilis is a mortal
human being, and if sent to his death, his name will soon be
forgotten. However, his sentence will not be forgotten. It will linger
on as an unerasable blot on Russian jurisprudence.

You have been told that the Jews are our enemies, that they
scorn us, treat us as subhumans. Do not be swayed by this, for if you
convict him regardless of the evidence, if he becomes a scapegoat
for our sins, or the sins of others, there will probably be people who
will—in the short run—applaud your verdict. In the long run, however, your verdict will be regarded as a regrettable aberration, a sad
page in the history of our judicial system.

9

**Oscar Gruzenberg's
Closing Argument
for the Defense**
October 25 and 26, 1913

Members of the jury, ritual murders, the use of human blood, a horrible accusation, frightening words long entombed in ancient history, rise again from the graves and infect the living. People who live peacefully side by side, know each other, suddenly become enemies. And when I stand before you and wish to speak to you about this awesome accusation leveled against the Jewish people, Jewish religion, or various religious sects, I don't know whether I can still merit your confidence, or earn your attention. What of it, if I grew up among you, was educated in your schools, studied your books, enjoyed the friendship of Christians . . . what of it, if I shared in your travails, your pains and misfortunes? Strange as it may seem, the clock of history has been turned back with a vengeance, and I find myself confronted with a frightening accusation, a resuscitated covenant of blood, which rends us apart and turns us into enemies. Some may think that my words are intended to drown out the death throes of the unfortunate boy, Andrey; but that is farthest from my mind. It is your prerogative to believe me or not.

Yet, if I had entertained the slightest notion, or harbored the thought that the Jewish religion, Jewish customs, allow or sanction the shedding of human blood, I would leave that faith without a moment's hesitation. I say it loud and clear in the full knowledge that my words will become known to Jews throughout the world. I am convinced, however, without a shadow of a doubt, that such crimes run counter to Jewish religious teachings and are abhorrent to Jews everywhere. An attempt has been made at this trial to take us to ancient, moss-covered graveyards in order to exhume three-thousand-year-old myths. This expedition into antiquity was meant to show whether the early Hebrews behaved cruelly toward the Amalekites, or other such tribes with whom they were at war, and whether Beilis should be held accountable for these primordial misdeeds. The presiding judge explained to you that the Jewish religion per se is not on trial, the court being only concerned with individual fanatics. According to this ruling, we have wasted three days on matters that have no bearing on this case. Yet what did we examine, what did we discuss these last three days? We delved into the Bible, the Talmud, the Zohar, books that were not authored by fanatics. These volumes represent Jewish religious thought, and we did it all for nothing.

You have heard from the prosecutor and one of the civil accusers, they summoned you to do what? They called on you not to punish the guilty on the basis of sound evidence, but as a consolation to the grieving mother of the dead boy. Yes, the unfortunate mother needs and deserves a word of solace and commiseration; but she certainly does not need, nor expects, a sacrificial offering to assuage her grief, or the conviction of an innocent man. I beg you to refresh your memory how she appeared before us in this courtroom. When I asked, "Whom do you suspect?" this saintly, simple woman uttered not a word against Beilis, not a word of accusation against Jews. At that moment, she had risen above the clamor for blind revenge, she had no desire to implicate the innocent in the loss of her son.

Alongside this tragic woman, there is another woman worthy of your attention and sympathy. That is Beilis's wife and her family. Is this woman luckier, more fortunate than Alexandra Prihodko? Doesn't this lonely, helpless, forsaken woman deserve your sympathy, your compassion? Take a look at this poor, honest, working family, whose life over these two and a half years has been transformed into a veritable nightmare.

What do you know about this man, Beilis? There has been a great deal of talk about Jews in the course of these proceedings—a variety of opinions about their qualities and characteristics. Surely, this particular Jew, a poor, honest toiler, working endless hours from sunrise to sunset, has earned the esteem, the empathy of his Christian co-workers, indeed, the goodwill of every Christian who takes the measure of a man by his work, his honesty, his life-style. You have seen these simple, earthy Christian workers, who worked alongside of Beilis day in and day out.Did they utter one derogatory word against Beilis?

We have seen the children who passed before us. There was this one moving moment when little Eugenia Voloshchenko was asked, "Did he ever chase you, offend you?" She smiled and said: "No, he never offended me, or hurt my feelings."

Still Beilis finds himself as the defendant in this case, languishing in prison these two and a half years—weary, crushed, lonely, a man who is being held accountable for skewed biblical interpretations, for texts dredged up from "dead" religious books, unfamiliar to most Jews, books that the vast majority of Jews had never seen or heard of.

He is being accused on the basis of evidence offered by inebriated trollops, by Volkivna, who was brought here after the authorities had combed every bar in town to find her, by Shachovsky, who changed his testimony seventeen times, and by a motley assortment of derelicts and thieves. It defies comprehension how a man could be sentenced to long imprisonment at hard labor on the basis of such flimsy, conflicting, and uncorroborated evidence.

You've heard the theory advanced by the prosecutor and the civil accusers to the effect that the chapel attached to the poorhouse, which was erected on the Zaitsev estate, required human blood for its consecration. If the accusers are serious in propounding this theory, why don't they act on their convictions, why don't they ascertain who built the chapel, who supervised its construction? The builder of the chapel is known, he appeared before us. He is Mark Zaitsev, the son of the late Jonas Zaitsev, the millionaire. If he required human blood to sanctify the chapel, why don't you hold him accountable, why don't you question him and all those who donated money to make this project possible? Shouldn't they all be defendants in this case? The reason they have not been charged is because you know full well that your theory doesn't have a leg to stand on.

Let's focus our attention on the bill of particulars incorporated in the Beilis indictment. The way this document was drafted defies judicial practice. The prosecutor claimed that Vera Cheberyak was without a doubt an accessory to the crime. He declared that "the voice of the people is the voice of God." The prosecution had intimated that "Cheberyak sold Andrey to the 'Yids'."

Mr. Shamkov gave this version a different twist, arguing, "Why either Beilis or Cheberyak, why not both Beilis and Cheberyak?" Whoever uttered these words exonerated Beilis.

For if Cheberyak was in cahoots with Jews, if she "sold" the unfortunate boy to the Jews, why the much-touted pilgrimage to Kharkov?

If she was in collusion with Jews, as the prosecutor claimed, the trip to Kharkov to meet Margolin was a senseless, ludicrous exercise in self-deception. Only Zamislovski, an experienced jurist, understood that anyone accepting the premise that Cheberyak is a participant in the crime automatically demolishes the indictment against Beilis. I believe Zamislovski's arguments are flawed, but I must admit that there were no inconsistencies or contradictions in his line of reasoning. The prosecutor argued that Cheberyak had been in collusion with unnamed Jews, and that she turned the boy over to them. But he apparently forgot that two-thirds of his speech was devoted to a characterization of Vera Cheberyak. He said she was a thief, that she maintained a den for unsavory characters. But, members of the jury, there is a considerable distance between being a woman of easy virtue with a penchant for young lovers and being a murderess. Yet the prosecutor negotiated that distance in an hour and a half, for after the recess, he lowered the boom on Cheberyak, conceding that she was a collaborator in the murder. Has something transpired during the recess to change the prosecutor's mind? To compound his inconsistency, the prosecutor embellished his charge with the hypothesis that perhaps Feivel Shneerson was also involved.

At this point, Mr. Zamislovski also overstepped the bounds of credibility. He said that the crime was premeditated, carefully planned in advance. The flaw in this reasoning is that the whole scenario hinged on whether Andrey would visit Zhenya on that particular Sunday. If he visits him, fine; if he doesn't, Jews will be deprived of their sacrificial offering, they'll be left without the prescribed quota of blood to consummate the ritual. Yet suppose the youngsters changed their mind? It is claimed that Zhenya managed to escape, but Andrey didn't. Is it not conceivable that it could have been the other way around—that Andrey fled, but Zhenya didn't? Could this be considered a premeditated crime? Would Jews risk provoking a pogrom with its devastating consequences, would rabbis and other religious functionaries be summoned from abroad to witness—what? Whether the boy will be caught or manage to flee? This is the glaring flaw in the indictment.

Of course, Mr. Zamislovski weighed in with the proposition that the likelihood of Feivel Shneerson luring the boy to the estate with the promise of taking him to see his long-vanished father cannot be discounted. If this were so, why implicate Vera Cheberyak? Why not make Shneerson accountable for his misdeed?

The prosecutors' statements are replete with speculations as to who may have committed the crime, but they have yet to produce a definitive answer. Who did commit the crime?

You, members of the jury, will undoubtedly recall Cheberyak's fairy tale about her mysterious trip to Kharkov. I have been particularly intrigued by Cheberyak's assertion that, had she consented to the alleged proposal to accept responsibility for the crime upon herself, she would be defended by the "greatest lawyers." And, indeed, Cheberyak is presently being defended by a team of distinguished lawyers, who are arrayed against us as members of the prosecution. Not only are these men skillful and experienced jurists, but they have at their disposal the full power and resources of the state. Although the prosecutor—in the final segment of his speech— did concede the probability of her complicity in the boy's murder, he had repeatedly referred to her as a "witness," and when she stumbled in her testimony, reminded her that she was under no obligation to "incriminate" herself.

Throughout these proceedings, we have heard of many instances of the ineptitude and inefficiency of the police authorities. If there was one official whose testimony had withstood the test of credibility, it was that of Colonel Ivanove. When I questioned him about his opinion of Kirichenko, he replied that he could unhesitatingly vouch for Kirichenko's honesty and integrity. Kirichenko told us: "It was clear to me, that no matter where one probed and searched for clues about the murder, the tracks inevitably led to Vera Cheberyak." This was the testimony of a reliable public servant who devoted eight to ten months to this case. He also testified that when questioning Zhenya and the latter seemed ready to offer a response with regard to Andrey's last visit to their home, he, Kirichenko, noticed a sudden convulsive change in the boy's demeanor.

"I turned around and saw Vera Cheberyak making threatening gestures to the boy," said Kirichenko.

Gentlemen, do you still have any doubts that Andrey's coat remained at the Cheberyak flat? Aren't the facts clear and unmistakable in this regard? Why didn't she turn the coat over to the police?

The prosecutor argued that Vera was afraid to get involved in a "messy affair," but at that point, there was no "messy affair." At that time, there was only a "missing boy" and no foul play was indicated. Remember, the boy was killed on March twelfth, but Cheberyak knew nothing of the murder, having found out about it from the newspapers only on March twentieth. She held on to Andrey's coat because surrendering it to the authorities would inevitably tie her to the crime. In light of these incontrovertible facts, Mr. Zamislovski's claim that the murder tracks lead to the brick factory, and from there directly to the cave, is sheer fantasy. No, gentlemen of the jury, all the tracks lead not to the brick factory, but to the home of Vera Cheberyak. The evidence points unmistakably to a brutal homicide perpetrated by cruel people, criminals with long prison records, and not to a carefully planned murder by Jews for ritual purposes.

Consider the pillowcase found in the murdered boy's pocket, which, on examination, showed traces of blood and male semen. In light of what we know of the goings-on in the Cheberyak's den of iniquity, the trysts and orgies indulged in by the underworld characters frequenting her home, can there be any doubt that the blood- and semen-stained pillowcase came from Cheberyak's home? We've heard references to a pillowcase being stuffed into Andrey's mouth to stifle his shrieks when the assault began. Cheberyak obviously panicked for fear that the boy's cries would alarm her neighbors, who, in turn, would summon the police.

If this were a ritual murder executed by Jews, is it conceivable that a dirty, semen-stained pillowcase would be used in a ritual rite which, according to those advancing this theory, required that the corpse be thoroughly washed while rabbis recited appropriate prayers? Surely the use of such impurity would have been incompatible with the solemnity of the occasion.

The prosecutor found it incomprehensible that the indictment of one Jew, Beilis, would precipitate such widespread concern and agitation among Jews. Yet the accusation against Beilis, the Jew, had snowballed into an indictment of all Jews.

The prosecuting team minced no words in casting a pall of suspicion upon Jewish practices and beliefs, and an array of religious experts had been summoned to probe and dissect Jewish religious books and customs in support of the long-discredited allegations against Jews and Judaism. You have all heard the testimony of Troyitsky, professor of the Theological Academy, a

man who has earned accreditation by the Holy Synod, a teacher
who had trained thousands of priests and had acquired a reputation
as a prodigious scholar. When questioned by the civil prosecutor, he
said: "I would be at a loss to understand if Jews, whose faith is being
questioned, whose holy books are under attack, would not react
collectively in defense of their religion." What he forgot to say was
that this calumny had plagued and tormented the Jewish people for
centuries and had exacted a heavy toll in lives and property.
Whether the accusation is leveled against all Jews or only against
some of them is immaterial. No Jew knows when lightning will
strike and who will be the victim.

The accuser admitted that he is unfamiliar with Jewish religious
books and that he is no authority on the subject, but he believes in
ritual murders on the basis of two or three books he had occasion to
read. Gentlemen of the jury, one may believe in goodness, in
beauty, in heaven, but one cannot entertain a belief in something
he knows nothing about.

For many centuries, we have lived and died under the crushing
weight of this slanderous accusation. And what had been done to
examine the validity of this libel?

The world boasts of great universities, science academies, research centers; there are scholars who are fluent in the Hebrew
language, who studied Jewish religious books in the original;
Kokovtsev is a prime example. This spiritual, ethereal personality,
known as the foremost Hebraist in all of Europe, these scholars are
constantly searching for the truth, they travel to distant lands to
explore the life and mores of ancient civilizations. I declare, without
fear of contradiction, that in the last two hundred years there were
no trials or disputations confirming the veracity of this accusation,
nor have I seen an accredited church scholar, be he Catholic, Greek
Orthodox, Lutheran, or Jew, who had validated or substantiated
this monstrous fairy tale . . .

PRESIDING JUDGE: You are offering testimony . . .

GRUZENBERG: But we've heard testimony from experts. I reit-
erate that there were no such trials, except in the Middle Ages

when people were tortured and executed without proof, when witches were tried on the evidence of voodoo healers, when summonses were sent to dogs and rats . . .

PRESIDING JUDGE: This is inadmissible . . . you are an experienced jurist, and I hesitate to interrupt you. However, I must intervene when there is a breach of proper court decorum.

GRUZENBERG: I am sorry, but we've heard three days of expert testimony—how in ancient times people had judged animals, wasting our time on such nonsense, and I have every right to refer to this pseudoscientific balderdash. Mr. Shmakov, in interrogating Pranaitis, took the Bible apart, slandering it as sanctioning cruelty, unbridled hate against human beings, and the use of human blood. And Pranaitis, coming up with the answers, or remaining mute . . . All this transpired before our very eyes. I thought to myself, God Almighty, is it possible, is it conceivable that the God of the Bible, who is equally holy to all religions, who is equally revered by Christians and Jews, has been suddenly transformed into a Jew from Kiev who is being hounded . . .

PRESIDING JUDGE: Mr. Defender, that is an insulting analogy. You are free to speak, but don't make such unacceptable comparisons.

GRUZENBERG: There was an all-out assault on the Bible, selective quotations, words out of context, biblical passages that are being recited in the temples of all religions, whether Catholic, Lutheran, Greek Orthodox, or Jewish—such blasphemies are unheard of, especially in a court of law.

The Jewish religion needs no defense. I am comforted, however, by the testimony of the Christian scholars who appeared before us, including Greek Orthodox scholars of impeccable scholarly credentials who unanimously refuted these calumnies against the Jewish religion. Let those who experience the same pain and agony as I do remember that the Greek Orthodox Church treats Jews fairly and graciously and has found nothing sinister or objectionable in Jewish religious books and laws of conduct.

10

G. G. Zamislovski's Closing Argument for the Prosecution
October 27, 1913

Your honor and members of the jury, the prosecutor, in his presentation, illuminated this case so well, that I will try to analyze only the factual evidence relevant to these proceedings. I will first refer to those accounts where innocent people were needlessly suspected. You will ask, what difference does it now make that these initial versions of the investigation turned up nothing of importance? These accounts are of interest not because they established the innocence of these individuals, but because they throw light upon the judgment and minds of the investigators. They are relevant because they show that the chief of the criminal investigation department, Mishchuk, and another chief, Krasovsky, led the investigation in a deliberately wrong direction. Mistakes, of course, are always possible, especially in such a complex case as this. However, I insist that these were not tactical mistakes, but a deliberate course of action. Such inhumane, indeed, criminal methods were used, that it seems obvious that an invisible, secret hand guided the investigation. This is where I find the initial version of the

investigation meaningful, in that there was no basis in suspecting
Alexandra Yushchinsky, that to suspect her was an absurdity, since
it was obvious that she could not have participated in the crime. But
the investigation was not only steered in the wrong direction, it
became increasingly inhumane and cruel. You've heard what was
done to Alexandra Yushchinsky, how she was arrested after the
boy's death, how she was not allowed to attend the funeral, how the
rumors spread against her, which turned the mob on her, how she
was tormented, she, who has just lost her firstborn so tragically, she,
who was in the fifth month of pregnancy. It was equally obvious that
there was no evidence against Fedor Nezhinsky, nor against Luka
Prihodko. In the Luka Prihodko episode, Mishchuk was no longer
involved, as his assignment was terminated. Krasovsky was now in
charge, and I deem it worthwhile to say a few words—not to
exonerate Prihodko, his innocence is self-evident—but to examine
Krasovsky's credibility. As to the evidence against Luka Prihodko, a
note was found with the words "temple bone." Prihodko is a bookbinder by trade and had on hand many book covers and notes. His
practice was to remove all notes from books and throw them in a
pile. From that pile, Krasovsky pulled one note with the inscription
"temple bone." When Prihodko argued, "I can identify the customer
whose book this note came from, approach him, and ask,"
Krasovsky refused to follow up.

Prihodko was then subjected to the indignity of a new makeup,
his beard was shaved, his mustache was darkened. Krasovsky does
not dispute it. He said he wanted him to look like he did at the time
of his first arrest. We thus have a fully verified falsification effected
on a human being. While Mishchuk used material for the forgery,
Krasovsky used a human being. Consequently, I cannot trust
Krasovsky's testimony. You will recall that Krasovsky was invited
to take part in the investigation when Mishchuk's actions became
suspect. Mishchuk did not want to go to Lukyanovka, he wanted to
stay away from Lukyanovka. When Krasovsky became involved,
he wanted to gain the trust of his superiors, he had to go to
Lukyanovka, but he was essentially doing it for his own private

reasons so he could use the uncovered evidence for his own purposes.

Krasovsky's duplicity was established—not based on rumors, but on fully documented facts. The prosecutor pointed out that Krasovsky's investigation in July proved that the murder took place at the factory. This was in July; but he was forced to admit that at the end of May he said in a report to the governor-general that the murder was committed by robbers. Krasovsky admits that he was telling Golubev that it was a ritual murder, but then he said he only did it to get rid of him, because Golubev and his associate would not hear of anything else. "They are fanatics," he said, "so I told them what they wanted to hear." This duplicity again points to an invisible hand which directs him and Mishchuk to commit forgeries. Krasovsky told us that he followed up every clue, that he visited Cheberyak and the factory. However, the results are aimed in one direction—only Christians are being arrested, while the Jews are untouched. Christians are being arrested without any evidence, but Prihodko—well, Krasovsky found a "mysterious" note in this possession, and somebody supposedly identified him, but what about Luka's brother, who was also arrested, and Luka's father was arrested, an old, half-blind man. Why? It looks like an act of vengeance to me.

When searching the factory, the investigator reported that some books were confiscated at Beilis's home, causing some concern and anxiety among the Jews, inasmuch as the books had some note in them. Krasovsky kept these books for several days, then turned them over to the prosecutor, who had not found anything suspicious in them. The question arises: were these the same books that were confiscated? There is, as you see, a serious question with regard to Krasovsky's honesty and credibility. His intention was not to reveal, but to hide the evidence; this is not merely an assumption, but a belief in facts.

After Mishchuk and Krasovsky were removed from the formal investigation, the volunteer detectives entered the case. Brazul and company, of the *Kievskaya Mysel* fame, were doing their investi-

gating in the shadows, behind the stage. While Mishchuk and
Krasovsky were the official investigators, the gentlemen of the
above-mentioned newspaper were useful as witnesses only. But
after their removal, there were no more officials left who closed
their eyes to the doings of the Jews.

Now, the moonlighting detectives had to come forward. The first
thing they did was to travel to Kharkov. Until then, things were
relatively cut-and-dry. Now Cheberyak is saying one thing, while
Margolin and Brazul are saying something else. Who is to be
believed? We must admit Cheberyak cannot be trusted. On the
other hand, we have a company of very trustworthy people. They
would appear to deserve more trust than Cheberyak. She claims
that they promised her 40,000 rubles, the best defense lawyers, new
documents (so that no one could find her)—so long as she admitted
her guilt in the crime. They claim that all of this is rubbish, that she
herself begged to be taken to Kharkov so that she could give
testimony and tell the truth. We need to figure out whether Margolin and Brazul are telling the truth, and as it turns out, they are
not. There are inconsistencies in their stories. They went to
Kharkov because Cheberyak asked them to; she said, "Let's go, I'll
give you the information," and so they went. But along with this
confidence in her, they showed mistrust. They took Perechrist with
them to watch over her, since they didn't trust her. Margolin, on his
arrival in Kharkov, did not register and was hiding. He said he was
hiding from Cheberyak, since her company might compromise him.
The facts show that he was hiding from the authorities, but later,
confirming that he did go to Kharkov, he produced a registration
form, which must have been back dated.

Thus, these gentlemen are not as truthful as it may seem, they are
hiding something. Then, not only Margolin and Brazul are telling us
about the trip to Kharkov, but also Krasovsky. He states that
Margolin told Cheberyak that all progressively thinking Russian
people would like to see the blood libel refuted and repudiated, and
that if she were to work in that direction, she would get paid.
Krasovsky is smarter than Brazul; he admits the facts instead of

denying them; he cleans them up, changes them around so that the facts look innocuous. That's how he describes the matter with the reward. In any case, he contradicts Brazul, who said that no one even mentioned a reward.

These contradictions show that although Cheberyak is a thief and runs a hangout for thieves, this time she is telling the truth. The same applies to the documents in question. Brazul and Margolin deny any references to documents, while Krasovsky admits that they talked about them, but hypothetically; in the event Cheberyak is menaced by criminals, they would help her escape. It is obvious that the purpose of the trip to Kharkov was to talk Cheberyak into admitting her guilt. The final version deals with the allegation that the murder took place at Cheberyak's flat. On March twelfth, in come Singayevsky, Rudzinsky, and Latyshev, Andrey follows, and was killed there. It seems that those who wanted to divert attention from the Jews were anxious to offer the authorities something believable; surely to argue that Cheberyak was the murderer was more probable and believable than to accuse Alexandra and Luka Prihodko. The version with Cheberyak came up back in March 1912, and it was a plausible way to shield the Jews and project a version that is likely to be more believable.

Therein lies the rub: had the versions implicating Cheberyak failed, the evidence against the factory Jews and against Beilis would assume greater credibility. It would then follow that the boy was killed at the factory. That is why the defense waited a whole year to come up with this version.

On March eighth, Cheberyak is caught with stolen goods, on March ninth, several underworld ringleaders are arrested, on March tenth, Cheberyak's flat is searched. Everyone is unnerved and apprehensive—the Cheberyak hangout is compromised. There were rumors that everything stolen in Kiev was hidden there. Who betrayed the thieves? Turns out that it was Andrey Yushchinsky, who planned to rob the Sophist Cathedral and who habitually slept at the Cheberyak flat. He had to be disposed of. At this point, the Dyakonovs showed up. They see everything: the panic and the murderers. What the Dyakonov sisters had seen, the Malitsky woman had heard. Everyone confesses—Cheberyak to the Dyakonovs, Singayevsky to Machalin and Karayev, Rudzinsky to Schwechko. Unique is the richness of this evidence, this picture is painted with the bold strokes of a great master. Something akin to an elaborate mechanism, where every wheel is meticulously crafted and meshed. Its beauty is in its smooth operation, which also has a reverse side—should one wheel fall out, the whole mechanism falls apart. Let's look at the facts.

The central figures here are the Dyakonovs, whose behavior does not inspire trust. These "girlies" frequent restaurants with Krasovsky, not knowing him well enough, drink wine, spend time, almost to midnight. One of them is wont to visit Colonel Ivanove to inform him of what's going on. Next time around, she would answer questions as to what happened in the past, nothing about new developments. Even Krasovsky admitted that when they deem it beneficial to them, they are apt to falsify the evidence. In the course of cross-examination, she had admitted five times that she had made a mistake during the preliminary investigation.

The Malitsky woman had heard everything others had seen. At first, she kept on saying that she did not know a thing, but later— after being tutored—she started to talk. Her teachers did not do a good job, though, as her testimony is full of contradictions. Everything in her testimony turned out to be a fabrication.

Shwechko told us a story of hearing how Rudzinsky admitted murdering Andrey. Supposedly, he heard it after being arrested and put in the same cell as Rudzinsky. Why he was arrested, we don't know. When Krasovsky told us that Andrey was planning to rob the Sophist Cathedral, he pointed to Shwechko as the source of his information, but Shwechko did not confirm it. Then, Krasovsky "remembered" that it was Brazul who told him that, and that Brazul got his information from Shwechko. Now the three men cannot agree on anything.

Shwechko told us that Rudzinsky admitted his guilt. It was then necessary to secure Singayevsky's confession, which Machalin said that he did. We have seen this young man, who although jailed at age seventeen, was found not guilty. He did not waste his time in prison, having mastered the language of the thieves. He said he was preparing for a singing career in opera. How did he get involved? He got involved in 1912, presumably "to serve justice." Yet, Yushchinsky was killed in 1911. Why did he wait that long "to serve justice"? Even stranger in appearance is Karayev. He lived in the Caucasus. One needs a very good reason to leave his home and come to Kiev. He said he received a letter and thought it important enough to go to Kiev on account of his party involvement, but he would not disclose those reasons. As to how the two started their investigation is full of contradictions. Something does not click here: he was obviously summoned from the Caucasus for something other than "the cause of justice."

Machalin told us that he talked to Singayevsky for three to four hours, that he admitted everything and left for Moscow the same day. Karayev claimed that Singayevsky left for Moscow the next day. Here is an inconsistency that cannot be dismissed. Then Brazul said he was present, but according to Machalin, he was present only at the beginning.

Brazul asserts that according to Singayevsky, it was Rudzinsky who killed Andrey, but Machalin's and Karayev's account mentioned both Rudzinsky and Latyshev as the killers.

Let's return— for the last time—to the Cheberyak version. The accusations against her have been disproved. This version received a great deal of attention from the defense, but quite apart from its being a fabrication from beginning to end, it falls apart based on the following logical conclusions. First, there was no motive. To make some sense out of the sequence of events leading to the murder, the defense resorted to slander, claiming that Andrey was planning a robbery, that he often spent nights at Cheberyak's, and that he knew what the thieves were up to.

Even if we were to assume that the thieves killed him for betraying them, it is too far-fetched to be credible. Since the boy visited the Cheberyaks infrequently, what could he have known? It was said that he was killed to stir up hostility against the Jews and thus provoke a pogrom. An expert witness for the defense, Professor Bekhterev, testified that he does not think there was a preconceived notion to make the murder look ritualistic in character. If they were interested in provoking a pogrom, surely they would have "planted" some clues to implicate the Jews. Instead, they did nothing of the kind and left in a hurry. This leads me to the conviction that there was no motive. Another compelling reason indicating that Rudzinsky and Singayevsky could not have done it is the fact that they participated in a robbery on March twelfth and departed immediately for Moscow, where they were arrested celebrating in a tavern. It would be sheer madness for them to leave the body with Cheberyak at a time when the gang had been under close surveillance and another search at the Cheberyak flat had been anticipated at any moment.

I apologize to the jury for taking so much time to disprove this theory of the murder, yet it was important to point out that the witnesses in support of this fiction gave false testimony, having been prompted by someone to "cook up" this version of the crime. What is the conclusion? Prior to the murder, the boy was seen between the brick factory and the Cheberyak flat. Since we established that he was not murdered at the Cheberyak home, it follows that it had to be at the factory. The boy's tracks, while still alive, lead to the factory right at the time of the crime, while the trail of the boy, now dead, lead from the factory grounds to the cave where his body was found. Isn't there reason enough to arrive at a single conclusion based on facts that the murder had, indeed, been committed at the factory? Yushchinsky reached the factory from Yurkovskaya Street, the part of the plant where Beilis lived, where Beilis is the boss. Given Beilis's position at the factory, this could not have happened without his knowledge. The collapse of the Cheberyak variant leads directly to Beilis; and those trying to protect the Jews knew it perfectly well; that is why the Cheberyak variant was used as a last resort.

The murder took place four hours after he ate borscht, according to professor Kosorotov, who said so. All experts agreed with that, except for professor Pavlov, who said it could have been four, or five, or six hours, but offered no proof of that. So we can confidently assume that it was four hours. When did he eat? He was seen at 6:05 to 6:10 by the bridge which is about fifteen to twenty minutes from the Yushchinsky home. He needed about ten minutes to dress, etc. He ate at 5:30 to 5:40. Since the medical experts fixed the time of his death some four hours after he ate, the murder must have taken place at 9:30 to 9:40 in the morning. Yushchinsky with Zhenya Cheberyak were seen by Shachovsky at 8:15, and 9:15 he was in the hands of his torturers. Now we have firmly established that just prior to the murder, Yushchinsky was near the factory grounds, in fact, at that part of the factory where Mendel Beilis is the boss. How do we know that he went to the factory? We have the testimony of Shachovsky, who heard it from Zhenya, and there is no reason to disbelieve him. You have all seen this pitiful, intimidated witness. He was obviously mistreated or beaten before he testified; hence, the direct witness testimony tells us that Yushchinsky went to the factory, and there is nothing to disprove it.

Zhenya Cheberyak told Golubev that Andrey visited him not long before his body was found, but he did not say that to the investigator. Why? Because of pressure from his mother. It had to be so. Had she told him to tell the truth, she would have followed her conscience, but she is not that kind of person. She is afraid to go against the factory Jews because they may disclose her connections with criminal elements. Hence, Zhenya's mouth was sealed, all the time, until he died. After Zhenya's death, the investigators called in Vassily Cheberyak, Zhenya's father and Vera's husband. Cheberyak, a former post office clerk, definitely told everything he knew, and his story was later confirmed by his daughter, Ludmilla. Based on the words of his children, he testified that they, the children, went to the factory grounds, the Jews attacked them, and Mendel Beilis caught Andrey. There is no reason to question the veracity of this testimony. Vassily is as different from his wife as water is from fire. It has been said that other witnesses did not corroborate this testimony. One girl, Dunya, said that they did go to the factory, played there, but no one attacked them.

Does this confirm or deny Ludmilla's testimony? Yes and no. Dunya told the truth about going to the factory, but she lied when she said that the Jews did not attack them.

There is a letter in the proceedings, written by Beilis to his wife and sent through one prisoner Kazachenko. This letter was intercepted. In the letter, Beilis indicated that he trusted the man. According to Kazachenko, Beilis asked him for help in poisoning Nakonechny and Shachovsky. For that, Kazachenko was supposed to have been paid. Is it possible that Kazachenko made it all up? Of the 200 witnesses we had before us, who could be the most harmful to Beilis? Nakonechny and Shachovsky, of course. Nakonechny could not have known that, and therefore had no reason to make up this story. Why was Nakonechny so important? Because his daughter, Dunya, saw everything, and if they both decided to tell the truth, it would have sunk Beilis. Yes, they both claimed that the Jews did not attack the children, and we don't know their reasons for lying; but were they to tell the truth, it would have seriously damaged Beilis. So he decided to kill the father. One could argue that if the murder was premeditated, the criminals would have acted pursuant to a plan. The children went to the factory, but they could have gone elsewhere, so how could a crime so delicate be left to chance? This is only a hypothetical contradiction.

The Jews knew that Andrey was going to be in or near the factory grounds on Saturday; they also knew that the boy yearned for his vanished father, so they invented one, "Uncle Pavel," who supposedly was in the Far East and who could easily lure the boy to go to the factory by promising to show him a letter or a photograph. After the children went to the factory, Zhenya was chased twice, and only dogs scared off the strangers. Yet Ludmilla saw a man who looked like Shneerson.

Let's say it was just a coincidence, where is the connection? But then there was another coincidence: the dogs that hindered the chase died later. Who knows whether they died on their own, or were poisoned? Then, another coincidence, which may or may not be related to something. After Beilis's arrest, Zhenya and Valentina Cheberyak died. Zhenya died of dysentery; was it a coincidence, or was he poisoned? On March tenth, horse stables and a barn burned down; another coincidence. We know that the horses, collars, harness, and Beilis's personal belongings were removed beforehand . . . Too many coincidences, don't you think?

Every factory inhabitant could account as to what he was doing on the premises, except for Shneerson. What kind of man is he? We know he is from Lubavich, the hotbed of Hasidism. From the Saratov affair, we know that blood was being sent to Lubavich. The only man living at the factory without a reason is linked to the Lubavich *tzadiks*, well known for their wild fanaticism. He said he never saw Andrey, but Olimpiada Nezhinsky said he knew the boy. Enough, already—these are not coincidences. Vassily Cheberyak testified, and Liuda confirmed, that prior to the murder, Zhenya and Liuda had seen at Mendel Beilis's place two strangely attired Jews. This took place at the time the foundation for the new synagogue was laid. Since the synagogue was being built at a different section of the factory grounds, the children, not knowing about it, could not have made it up. And whom did the two rabbis visit? The person who is close to Shneerson and the Lubavich *tzadiks*, and who is himself taking an active part in the rituals, namely Beilis. This is no coincidence; there is an experienced hand behind all of this. This factory was not only a place where bricks were made but also a place where Jews assembled—Shneerson is there, Beilis is there, the Lubavich rabbis visit there, where the synagogue they built secretly, unbeknown to the authorities, is located. I have every reason to believe that the boy was killed there and that it was Beilis who killed him.

A word about the medical examination. There were many experts involved in this investigation, and they have often disagreed with each other. We need to decide which of the experts deserves more attention. I think we should trust more the experts who did the postmortem examination firsthand. I would also value the experts in forensic medicine over those whose specialty is surgery. So the opinion of professors Obolonsky, Tufanov, and Kosorotov should merit our confidence. The experts say they found forty-seven wounds. Think of it, forty-seven! The killers obviously wanted to inflict pain, but they were not sadistic. All experts agree on that. We were also told that between five and five and one-half glasses of blood were extracted. The murder weapon was a stabbing tool. Why? Because, according to Jewish ritual, blood from a pricked wound does not have to be covered. We know this from Professor Troyitsky. Also, Andrey wore a hat; that's because Jews cover their heads during religious ceremonies. Further, there were thirteen wounds found on the boy's head. True, some argued that there were fourteen wounds; but those experts we decided to trust more say that the correct number is thirteen. Why these thirteen wounds? No one knows, since they were not needed to kill, nor to drain the blood, nor to torture. But as Professor Troyitsky told us, every good Jew, when he dies, reads a prayer, the essence of which is in the last word, *Ehad*, i.e., "the only one." According to the Torah, each word has a corresponding number, and *Ehad* corresponds to number thirteen.

Next let's look at the neck wounds. These are the wounds inflicted to drain the blood. To Jews, blood is of extreme importance, for that's where the soul is. When an animal is killed, his throat is cut. This shows that the murder had a ritual character. Inasmuch as Beilis was baking matzos, and Shneerson was from Lubavich where blood was being sent to, and that the synagogue chapel was sprinkled with blood, the facts add up to a ritual murder, and not to a coincidence. There is no doubt that the Old Testament stressed the importance of blood sacrifices, which represent the essence of Judaism.

The sacrifice ceremonies were conducted at the Temple in Jerusalem. Since the Temple was destroyed, the rites of sacrifices continue. The Jews' hatred for Christians is intensifying, as they were the ones who destroyed the Temple. Jewish religious books are replete with references to the *goy*, who is an abomination, and to kill a *goy* is permissible, even on the Sabbath. The scientific understanding of these books varies and is subject to different interpretations. Is it not possible, however, that Jewish fanatics interpreted these references as license to kill? There was a disputation that took place in the city of Lvov, where one group of Jews accused another group of ritual murders. Thereafter, a series of murders took place in Europe, all similar to the murder we are dealing with here. In Russia, in 1817, the Emperor Alexander I decreed that Jews are not to be persecuted for ritual murder without proof. It does not mean that he ruled out the existence of ritual murders, he just stipulated that these have to be proved. There were many cases of ritual murders during the reign of emperors Nicholas I and Alexander II. No one can deny that such murders had occurred, and here we have Beilis, who killed Andrey for religious motives. In this case, I am representing Alexandra Yushchinsky, but she is not the only one awaiting your verdict. All of Russia is looking to you for an affirmative decision.

11

The Verdict
Thirty-fourth Day of Trial
(October 28, 1913)

As the jury retired to consider the verdict, the mood among Beilis's defenders was gloomy. The presiding judge's summation—glaringly prejudicial to Beilis—deepened their dismay.

At twenty minutes to six, the foreman entered with unusual solemnity, holding in his hand the text of two questions. He read out the first question:

> Has it been proved that on March 12, 1911, in one of the buildings of the Zaitsev brick factory . . . Andrey Yushchinsky was gagged, and wounds inflicted on him . . . and that when he had lost five glasses of blood, other wounds were inflicted on him . . . and that these wounds totaling forty-seven caused Yushchinsky agonizing pain and led to almost total loss of blood and to his death?
>
> JURY FOREMAN: Yes, it has been proved.
>
> Is the accused, Mendel Teviev Beilis, guilty of having entered into collusion with others, who have not been discovered

in the investigation, in a premeditated plan prompted by
religious fanaticism to murder the boy Andrey Yushchinsky,
and did the accused in order to carry out his intentions, seize
Yushchinsky . . . and drag him off to one of the buildings of the
brick factory?

JURY FOREMAN: No. Not guilty.

The silence which enveloped the public during the reading of the
questions was shattered by prolonged cheers and applause when
the verdict was announced. Surrounded by a sea of well-wishers,
Beilis was in tears. A Russian merchant, shoving everyone aside,
embraced Beilis, shouting: "I let three factories in St. Petersburg,
while I sat here for a month. I couldn't go home. I couldn't have
slept. Now, thank God, I can go home a happy man."

A requiem mass for Yushchinsky planned by the Union of the
Russian People to coincide with the announcement of the verdict
was called off. Crestfallen, the anti-Semitic rabble dispersed silently.
There was rejoicing throughout the country. However, the festive
mood faded during the ensuing days. The rightist press disclosed
that on the question of Beilis's guilt, the jury was divided, six to six—
an acquittal under Russian law.

While Shcheglovitov and his cohorts suffered a crushing debacle,
they soon recovered to claim victory. They rationalized that while
Beilis was declared innocent of the crime, the religiously motivated
ritual-murder accusation was not demolished by the verdict. Commented the *Manchester Guardian*: "The humble jury had the
courage to at least acquit the Jew whom so many powerful influ-
ences had conspired to destroy. Unfortunately, their courage did
not carry them further, as they let stand the words in the verdict that
'the murder was committed on the grounds of the Zaitsev brick
factory.' "[1] To the consternation and strenuous objections of the
Beilis defense team, the two questions addressed to the jury were

---

1. Maurice Samuel, *Blood Accusation—The Strange History of the Beilis
Case* (Philadelphia: Jewish Publication Society, 1966), p. 251.

framed in such a way as to leave the religious motivation of the crime unaffected by the verdict. Nevertheless, world opinion—and large sections of Russian society—held that the gamble of the government to blacken the image of the Jew ended in a fiasco. Thus, the *Daily News* of London wrote: "The acquittal of Beilis was the most crushing blow to Russia since the Russo-Japanese war."[2] Anglo-Jewish historian Lucien Wolf commented: "I am afraid that we cannot congratulate ourselves on the result of the Kiev trial. There can be little doubt that the verdict was engineered by the authorities with the idea of throwing dust in the eyes of foreigners, while at the same time preserving the blood-accusation and even giving it a measure of countenance."[3]

Moreover, the government supporters in St. Petersburg threw a "victory party," at which Minister of Justice Shcheglovitov and prosecutor Vipper were the guests of honor. Zamislovski was rewarded with a gift of 25,000 rubles to write a book about the trial, and Boldyrev, the presiding judge, was promoted, as promised, and in addition received a gold watch from the czar.

Domestic Reaction

In Russia itself, the progressive elements, the intelligentsia, the academic community, and the liberal press felt affronted by the Beilis "spectacle" that the czarist government staged and presented to the eyes of the world. A large number of newspapers and academic journals were confiscated for denouncing the spuriousness of the trial. The liberal press had claimed from the very beginning that czarist officialdom knew all along who the murderers of the boy Yushchinsky were, and that the real culprits were

---

2. Samuel, *Blood Accusation*, p. 252.
3. Ibid., p. 253.

being shielded from prosecution in order to "prove" the validity of the blood-libel accusation. A Russian manifesto issued over the signatures of leading personalities in arts, science, law, and politics, including such notables as Korolenko, Gorky, Count Ilya Tolsoy, six members of the Imperial Council, and sixty-four members of the Duma, declared, inter alia: "The eternal struggle of humanity for liberty, legal equality and fraternity and against slavery, hate and social discord have been with us since ancient times. And in our times, as always, the same persons who uphold the rightless condition of their own people are the most persistent in stirring up the spirit of religious and racial enmity. The false story of the use of Christian blood by Jews has been broadcast once more among the people. This is a familiar device of ancient fanaticism."[4]

World Reaction

The Beilis trial evoked a tidal wave of criticism and condemnation throughout the civilized world. As the early reports of developments reached the West, press comments were couched in terms of disbelief. Thus, the *New York Times* commentator observed: "This case reminds one of the farmer who saw a camel and said 'there ain't no such animal'."[5] As the trial progressed, the first expression of dismay and condemnation came from Germany. It was signed by 206 well-known personalities, among them Thomas Mann, Gerhard Hauptmann, Herman Sudermann, and Werner Sombart. The British weighed in with a statement endorsed by the archbishops of Canterbury and York, the primate of Ireland, Francis Cardinal Bourne, the speaker of the House of Commons, and prominent members of both houses of Parliament, including

---

4. Samuel, *Blood Accusation*, p. 242.
5. Samuel, *Blood Accusation*, p. 231.

A. J. Balfour, Austin Chamberlain, and Ramsay MacDonald. Among Britain's literary greats, the signers were Thomas Hardy, H. G. Wells, and E. G. Pointer, president of the Royal Academy. The French protest was endorsed by the heads of France's highest institutions of learning plus such notables as Anatole France, Henri de Regnier, and Octav Mirbeau. The first American statement of protest was signed by 74 leaders of various Christian denominations. The almost universal expressions of protest and condemnation were soon followed by mass meetings in England, Germany, France, the United States, Canada, and Austria-Hungary. There were demonstrations in London and the major cities of the United States and Canada. A lead article in the influential *Manchester Guardian* blasted the czarist government, stating that "the administration of the country is in a hopeless and chaotic condition, without any guiding principle, but a blind dread of revolution."[6] The *Frankfurter Zeitung* referred to the trial as "a comedy, scarcely overshadowed the genuine tragedy . . . a lunatic asylum."[7] The liberal *Neue Freie Presse* of Vienna asserted that the "trial recalls the most miserable examples of classical Russian trials . . ."[8] The *London Times* observed: "Who would have supposed that in the 20th Century . . . we should see a court solemnly discussing Black Magic, Moloch, what Dio Cassius said, what Julian the Apostate did, and whether Jews drink Christian blood to counter a divine curse on their anatomy . . ."[9]

The most telling reaction came from New York's newspaper, the *Independent*, which was in the form of an open letter to Czar Nicholas. "When you ascended the throne of the Russian Empire, the expectations of your people ran high. They were yearning for reforms, for a sympathetic bond between the palace and the hovels of the hungry. . . . little by little the vision of a better day faded . . . you have gone much farther than your father in your anti-Jewish

---

6. Ibid., p. 233.
7. Samuel, *Blood Accusation*, p. 233.
8. Ibid., p. 234.
9. Ibid., p. 235.

policies. To divert attention from their own incompetence, your officials are pointing to the Jews as the cause of all the troubles that exist in Russia, and now to add to the crown of your infamy, your Minister of Justice has staged a 'ritual murder' case. How can you, the man who suggested the establishment of universal peace, tolerate such refinement of barbarity and brutality? How can you expect to face your Maker with such a burden on your soul?"[10]

Not all statements emanating from European countries were uniformly critical of the czarist regime. In France, individual figures associated with the discredited royalist cause raised their voices in support of the Russian government's handling of the trial and against the "Jew-inspired" agitation in defense of Beilis. Some newspapers, while questioning the legal basis of the trial, cautioned against "meddling" in the internal affairs of a "friendly country." Thus, W. T. Stead, writing in the "Review of Reviews," while disclaiming any anti-Jewish bias, cautioned the Jews "that they may give a dangerous impetus to anti-Semitism if they persist in subordinating the interests of general peace to pursuit of their vendetta with Russia."[11]

Russian diplomats accredited to Western countries sought to minimize or discredit the criticism of the Russian regime. Baron Heiking, the consul-general in London, wrote in the *Fortnightly Review*: "They (the Jews) feel themselves to be foreigners among the population of the land in which they dwell and strangers to its natural aims . . . they have but one leading idea—to strive for their own narrow, tribal purposes."[12]

In a commentary in the *London Times*, the same diplomat asserted that "the accusation of the ritual murder of the boy Yushchinsky is not at all leveled against Judaism and the Jewish people, but only the accused, who is believed to belong to a small

---

10. Ibid.
11. Samuel, *Blood Accusation*, p. 238.
12. Ibid., p. 240.

sect carrying the Talmudic teaching to the extreme ritual murder."[13]

Bakhmetev, Russia's ambassador to the United States, wired home that "the American 'Yids' have not failed to take advantage of the opportunity and have used the Kiev case to foment a new agitation against Russia . . . Congressman (Adolph J.) Sabath, a Yid, has presented a resolution demanding that the Secretary of State convey to His Majesty the expression of the feelings of indignation of the American people. Senator (Hamilton) Lewis has done the same in the Senate."[14]

In a similar vein, the chief of police Beletsky, himself a suborner and active participant in the "staging" of the Beilis trial, wrote to his superior, the minister of the interior: "Not confining themselves to insinuations against the Russian government and Russian justice, the Jews—in their hatred—have made it their task to attribute responsibility for the trial to the personal anti-Semitic feelings of the Supreme Power (the czar)."[15]

A revealing insight into the sordid backstage maneuvers surrounding the trial was provided by Russia's ambassador to the Vatican, Nelidov. Lord Rothschild of London wrote to the Vatican requesting written verification of papal bulls repudiating the blood accusation against Jews. Cardinal Merry del Val, papal secretary of state, complied with Lord Rothschild's request, but in order to transmit the Vatican's written response to Russia for presentation at the trial, it was necessary that the signature of Cardinal del Val be authenticated by the Russian embassy at the Vatican. To bolster the prosecution's case at the trial, and to please his superiors, ambassador Nelidov purposely delayed authenticating the cardinal's signature until the Beilis case was over. In a letter to his superior, Russia's minister of foreign affairs, S. D. Sazanoff, Nelidov bragged

---

13. Ibid., pp. 240–241.
14. Samuel, *Blood Accusation*, p. 241.
15. Ibid.

about his clever ruse. "I agreed to transmit the document," he wrote, "provided the word 'duplicate' was inscribed on it. When this was done, the copy could no longer have any significance for it could not reach Kiev until after the announcement of the verdict in the Beilis case."[16]

Minister Sazanoff thought well enough of Nelidov's "resourcefulness" to bring it to the attention of the czar.

The Beilis defense team had strenuously sought the Vatican document in order to refute the testimony of the religious expert Pranaitis, who had argued that the papal statements "absolving Jews of the ritual murder accusation were 'forgeries'." Had the Vatican document confirming the authenticity of the papal bulls reached the courtroom in time, the defense would have been able to discredit Pranaitis's testimony and refute his "expertise."

---

16. Samuel, *Blood Accusation*, p. 242.

Epilogue

In the aftermath of the 1917 revolution, justice had finally caught up with some of the players in the Beilis conspiracy. While the record is sketchy, the proceedings of the investigating commission set up by the provisional government and whatever archival data was made available since then revealed the following pertinent facts:

Shcheglovitov and Beletsky were shot by the Bolsheviks in 1918.

Vipper was tried by the revolutionary tribunal, and while the state prosecutor asked for the death penalty, Vipper escaped with a short prison sentence on account of his "usefulness" to the administration.

Golubev was killed in World War I, and Pranaitis died in St. Petersburg in 1917.

Vera Cheberyak and her half-brother, Singayevsky, were shot by the Bolsheviks in 1918. Confirmation of Cheberyak's execution is attributed to journalist, Chaim Shoshkess, who in an article in the Yiddish daily *Der Tog-Morgen Journal* of December 1, 1963, re-

225

ported as follows: "While a prisoner of the Bolsheviks in Kharkov in 1920, he heard the Warden, Anteszersky, tell a group of prisoners that he himself had shot Cheberyak in the Cheka prison in Kiev."[1]

Mendel Beilis left Russia in 1914, and with the financial aid of a few admirers, settled in Palestine. He acquired a home in Petach-Tikva, but it subsequently burned down. The anticipated financial help from philanthropists in Paris, Berlin, and New York did not materialize, and life in Palestine—still under Turkish rule—was primitive and harsh. Beilis and his family moved to New York, where he published an account of his ordeals as a prisoner in Kiev in a volume entitled *The Story of My Sufferings*, which ran first in a Yiddish newspaper. With his celebrity status in decline, he died a disillusioned man in 1934.

With the advent of the Communist regime, Gruzenberg, Karabchevsky, and Margolin went into exile. Maklakov was appointed ambassador to France by the provisional government, but he never returned to Russia—he died in France in 1959.

Brazul-Brushkovsky was arrested during the purges in 1937, and his fate was never ascertained.

---

1. Maurice Samuel, *Blood Accusation—The Strange History of the Beilis Case* (Philadelphia: Jewish Publication Society, 1966), p. 254.

Appendix

The Beilis Trial Roster

Note: Over two hundred witnesses were called to testify at the trial. Below is a list of the major participants and witnesses:
Boldyrev, Feodor A., Presiding Judge

Prosecutors:
Vipper, O. V., State Prosecutor
Shmakov, S., Civil Prosecutor
Zamislovski, G. G., Civil Prosecutor, Member of the Imperial Duma

Defense Team:
Gruzenberg, Oscar, Head of Defense Team
Maklakov, V. A., Defense Lawyer, Member of Imperial Duma
Karabchevsky, N. B., Defense Lawyer
Also: A. S. Zarudny and D. N. Grigorevich-Barsky

The Criminal Trio:
Rudzinsky, Boris
Latyshev, Ivan
Singayevsky, Piotr

The Conspirators (not appearing at the trial):
Shcheglovitov, I. G., Minister of Justice
Beletsky, Stepan P., Director, Dept. of Police
Chaplinsky, State Prosecutor

Major Witnesses for the Prosecution:
Golubev, Vladimir
Cheberyak, Vera
Cheberyak, Vassily
Cheberyak, Ludmilla
Cheberyak, Zhenya
Shachovsky, Kazimir
Shachovsky, Yuliana
Kazachenko

Major Witnesses for the Defense:
Krasovsky, Nikolai
Brazul-Brushkovsky
Machalin, Sergei
Karayev, Amzor
Dyakonov, Katerina (also Katherine, Ekaterina)
Malitsky, Zinaida
Margolin, Arnold

Other Witnesses for the Prosecution:
Dobzansky
Ivanove, Pavel, Lt. Colonel,
Head of Kiev Gendarmery
Kirichenko, Police Captain
Miffle, Pavel, Cheberyak's former lover

Mishchuk, Chief of Kiev Secret Police
Nezhinsky, Natalia, Yushchinsky's aunt
Nezhinsky, Olimpiada, Yushchinsky's grandmother
Prihodko, Alexandra, Yushchinsky's mother
Prihodko, Luka, Yushchinsky's stepfather
Shneerson, Feivel
Priest Sinkevich

Other Witnesses for the Defense:
Zaitsev, B.
Vygranov
Polishchuk
Chachovsky
Fenenko

Medical Experts:
Karpinsky, Dr., City Coroner
Kosorotov, Prof. of Forensic Medicine
Sikorsky, Prof. of Psychology

Religious Experts:
Father Justin Pranaitis
Prof. Glagolev
Prof. Troyitsky
Prof. Kovovtsev
Rabbi Jacob Mazeh

Glossary

Black Hundred Shock-troops of the Union of the Russian People. Pogromists, rabble, "unhanged villains" (Count Witte)

Congress of the United Nobility Influential monarchist landowners; the backbone of the czarist political base

Double-Headed Eagle Local reactionary and anti-Semitic organization, surrogate of the Union of the Russian People

Hasid (Hasidism) Mystical, less-doctrinaire stream in Judaism; believe in serving God with joy

Kabbalah Book of Jewish mysticism

Kievskaya Mysel "The Kiev Idea," newspaper

Mitnaged (Mitnagdim) Opponents of Hasidism, more respectful of traditional rabbinic disciplines

Tzadik

"Righteous," applied to Hasidic rabbis, who were held as intermediaries between man and God and treated with reverence

Union of the Russian People

National, monarchist, anti-Semitic organization

Zohar

Central book of the Kabbalah

Bibliography

Baron, Salo W. *The Russian Jew Under Tsars and Soviets*. New York: Macmillan Publishing Co., 1926.

The Beilis Case. Stenographic Account. 3 vols. Kiev, 1913. Issued with permission of the editors of *Kievskaya Mysel*.

Bernstein, Herman. *The Truth About the "Protocols of Zion."* New York: Ktav Publishing House, 1971.

Dundes, Alan, ed. *The Blood Libel Legend—A Casebook in Anti-Semitic Folklore*. Madison, WI: The University of Wisconsin Press, 1991.

Flannery, Edward H. *The Anguish of the Jews*. New York: The Macmillan Co., London: Collier-Macmillan, 1965.

Friedman, Saul S. *The Incident of Massena*. New York: Stein and Day Publishers, 1978.

Lindemann, Albert S. *The Jew Accused—Three Anti-Semitic Affairs (Dreyfus, Beilis, Frank), 1894–1915*. Cambridge: Cambridge University Press, 1991.

Roth, Cecil, ed. *The Ritual Murder Libel and the Jew*. London: The Woburn Press, n.d.

Samuel, Maurice. *Blood Accusation—The Strange History of the Beilis Case*. Philadelphia: Jewish Publication Society, 1966.

Tager, Alexander B. *The Decay of Czarism—The Beilis Trial*. Philadelphia: Jewish Publication Society, 1935.

Index

About the Author

Ezekiel Leikin was born in Vilno (now Vilnius) and spent his early youth in Kazan, Russia, where his father, Dr. George Leikin, served as community rabbi. An avowed anti-Communist, Dr. Leikin fled to the United States just prior to the advent of the Bolsheviks.

In his teens, Leikin came under the influence of the Zionist leader Vladimir Jabotinsky, helped organize the "Betar" youth movement, and rose to leadership positions in the Zionist-Revisionist Organization of America, now known as "Herut." Leikin moved to Palestine in 1936, was employed by the Palestine (British) government, enlisted in the United States Army in 1943 at an American military base near Tel Aviv, and served with military intelligence in Egypt, North Africa, and Europe.

After the war, Leikin joined the professional staff of the Zionist Organization of America (ZOA), retiring in 1981. In 1980, Leikin was awarded ZOA's Brandeis Award for "exemplary service to Zionism and Israel." During the 1982 Israeli campaign in Lebanon, Leikin worked as consultant to Israel's Foreign Ministry's Information Department in Jerusalem for a period of four months.

Leikin has written and lectured extensively on Israel, Zionism, and the Middle East and is currently associated with the ZOA District in Metropolitan Detroit.